RADICAL
DISTORTION

RADICAL
DISTORTION

HOW EMOTIONS
WARP WHAT WE HEAR

JOHN W.
REICH

Prometheus Books

59 John Glenn Drive
Amherst, New York 14228–2119

Cover image © 2012 Media Bakery
Cover design by Grace M. Conti-Zilsberger

Inquiries should be addressed to
Prometheus Books
59 John Glenn Drive
Amherst, New York 14228–2119
VOICE: 716–691–0133
FAX: 716–691–0137
WWW.PROMETHEUSBOOKS.COM

16 15 14 13 12   5 4 3 2 1

Library of Congress Cataloging-in-Publication Data

Reich, John W., 1937–
    Radical distortion : how emotions warp what we hear / by John W. Reich.
        p. cm.
    Includes bibliographical references and index.
    ISBN 978–1–61614–658–0 (pbk. : alk. paper)
    ISBN 978–1–61614–659–7 (ebook)
    1. Emotions. 2. Attitude (Psychology) 3. Radicalism. 4. Social psychology.
I. Title.

BF511.R45 2012
302—dc23

                                                        2012018457

Printed in the United States of America on acid-free paper

To Deb, my wife and partner in life
To Charles, my older brother and role model for being a scientist
And a memorial to my two mentors, Muzafer Sherif and O. J. Harvey, pioneers in revealing the emotional core of human cognition

CONTENTS

ACKNOWLEDGMENTS

Writing a book is a complicated project, and only in retrospect can the author come to realize how many people have made so many different and significant contributions to the final product. Each contributor's effort shows up in this book in ways both distinctive and subtle, so I am happy to take this opportunity to tell the rest of the world how my own efforts have been aided by the friendship and cooperation of these people. My wife, Deborah Oldfield Reich, has been by my side with her skillful reading and commenting skills. Dr. Bill Uttal, psychologist and author of thirty-one books (and counting), has made numerous valuable suggestions. He and I belong to the Arizona State University Discussion Group on Critical Thinking, which also includes Dr. Robert Cialdini, Dr. Dale Kent, Dr. Barry Leshowitz, whose constant attention, support, and new thinking have been inspirational. With this group, I have been able to hone my thinking about the topics that constitute this book. Drs. Alex Zautra and Mary Davis have been constant companions in my attempts to meld social-psychological thinking with clinical psychology and with our new emphasis on adult resilience. Dr. Jim Hoffmeister is a role model of deep thinking and high levels of motivation. Ms. Elizabeth Lowry and Ms. Amanda Baraldi both contributed greatly to the technical side of my production efforts. Dr. Keith Crnic, chair of the Psychology Department at Arizona State University, has provided work space for me and a supportive administrative and intellectual atmosphere for a remarkable department of outstanding colleagues. Finally, my primary publishing support has been provided by Steven L. Mitchell, editor in chief of Prometheus Books, and his outstanding copyeditors, Julia DeGraf and Brian McMahon.

10 ACKNOWLEDGMENTS

The intensity of my gratitude to all these people is bordering on radical partisanship.

RADICAL SPEECH/RADICAL HEARING: WHY VOICESOF MODERATION CAN'T BE HEARD

I am writing this book in frustrating times. These days, everyone seems to be angry at someone or at some group belonging to "the enemy." National opinion surveys are showing that the majority of people say that they are unhappy with "the way things are going." This discontent is widespread, and it is destructive. Critical legislation cannot get passed, voting is contentious, religion-based and politics-based intolerance distorts public policy, and effective social action becomes difficult if not impossible. In the swirling of this vortex, voices that choose the path of reason, moderation, and accommodation are not being heard. Our society is being subjected to social forces that are trying to divide us from each other, to make us want to demonize and cast out anybody with different opinions. But our so-called opponents are in fact our fellow citizens; we are all living on the same planet, and no matter how we may wish it, no one can just "go away." Should we not all unite and try to solve our common problems together?

Let's see what we are dealing with here. I will present a number of radical, extremist quotations illuminating various points about social divisiveness that need to be examined. Right now, I want to provide just a few examples so you can get a feel for the magnitude of the problem. I have mainly selected quotes related to the topic of religion, since that is one of the hottest of the hot-button issues where our divisions seem to be so insurmountable.

Gary Potter, president of Catholics for Christian Political Action, has been quoted as saying, "When the Christian majority takes over this country, there will be no satanic churches, no more free distribution of pornography, no more talk of rights for homosexuals. After the Christian majority takes control, pluralism will be seen as immoral and evil and the state will not permit anybody the right to practice evil."[1]

Randall Terry, founder of the antiabortion organization Operation Rescue, has voiced thoughts similar in intent to those of Potter's. He has been quoted as saying, "I want you to just let a wave of intolerance wash over you. I want you to let a wave of hatred wash over you. Yes, hate is good. . . . Our goal is a Christian nation. We have a biblical duty, we are called by God, to conquer this country. We don't want equal time. We don't want pluralism."[2]

But there are many people on "the other side." Many public figures have spoken out against religion, per se. The brilliant inventor Thomas Edison is quoted as saying: "I have never seen the slightest scientific proof of the religious ideas of heaven and hell, of future life for individuals, or of a personal God . . . I do not believe that any type of religion should ever be introduced into the public schools of the United States."[3]

Two lionized figures central to the founding of the American nation show a radical disdain for organized religion. James Madison, among whose chief contributions was the development of the First Amendment to the Constitution (concerning freedom of religion, speech, and the press), said, "During almost fifteen centuries has the legal establishment of Christianity been on trial. What has been its fruits? More or less, in all places, pride and indolence in the clergy, ignorance and servility in the laity; in both, superstition, bigotry, and persecution."[4] Thomas Jefferson, who along with John Adams was key to the actual development and writing of the Constitution, thought that "religions are all alike—founded upon fables and mythologies."[5]

So, major fault lines have existed in American society from its beginning. The same is true of most societies. But the fault lines are now very serious, and social discontent is harming our sense of unity. Remember that we were founded as the *United* States of America. My real concern is that the forces of divisiveness and polarization are winning out and that moderate voices with the best chance to reunite us are often not even being presented in the public forum. Just look at your television and editorial pages for evidence of the domination of the news by dissension, dispute, and hostility. Of course, this dissension does not exist solely in American society. Historically, we have seen many bloody examples of "versus": Irish Catholics versus Irish Protestants; Palestinians versus Israelis; the English versus the French versus the Russians; Liberals versus Conservatives; Greenpeace versus Whalers, Labor versus Big Business—the list could go on and on, which may lead one to think that perhaps a major force in human history is "versus." It is a natural feature of the way we live our lives in social groupings.

But there is a way out. In this book, I will take a close look at the dynamic forces underlying this discontent. Perhaps surprisingly, these forces are well-understood: we know why people have such a difficult time in getting along with each other. From social-science research—particularly from social psychology research—we will find answers that might make you uncomfortable because they strike very close to home. The problem lies in our own mental processes: yours and mine. The danger to our society lies in our beliefs and attitudes and how they come into play when we deal with the beliefs and attitudes of other people. Research has repeatedly shown how concerned, rational, and intelligent people lose their ability to truly understand and appreciate each other when their attitudes and emotions become involved. The central problems, therefore, lie in the very bedrock of the way the human mind functions. It is in our emotions and their poisonous effects on our thinking and judgment processes that we find the seeds of narrow-mindedness, prejudice (prejudgment), and the consequent polarization of our society.

Throughout this book, I will present research evidence on various facets of how our divisive relationships arise and function. In these discussions, when appropriate, I will offer some everyday phrases and thoughts that characterize the principles I am discussing. Here are some examples: The classic American mottoes "Don't Tread on Me" and "Live Free or Die" are key components of our history, but they are tinged with a streak of aggressiveness and suggest a rejection of others. Other sayings, less lofty and more universal, carry a similar connotation: "My way or the highway," "If you're not with me, then you are against me," and, perhaps worse: "Don't bother me with facts, my mind is made up." The common theme expressed in these sayings is found in other, classic phrases cast at a different level: "My Country, Right or Wrong" expresses a sentiment deeply believed by many Americans. Compare this with the Nazi mantra "*Gott mit uns*" (God with us), which demonstrates the Nazi belief that God was on the side of Germany's drive to conquer the world.

In the big picture, our problem is not that people believe in their own personal or national superiority. (Later in the book, I call this "radical-*supporting* speech"—when people fervently believe in the truth and justice of their side.) We expect people to invest their own personal beliefs with emotional commitment, even to the point that they believe that God has chosen them for greatness. We may not agree with that person, but there is a general recognition in a democratic society that people can speak freely about their beliefs, and so we expect proud mothers to brag about their children, businesses to extol the virtues of their products, and patriots to praise their countries. No one likes a braggart, but bragging is not a social problem. The real problem arises when that kind of extreme speech belief goes beyond supporting the self and starts attacking someone else's child, some other business's product, or someone else's country. I call this "radical-*attacking* speech," and it is the core of our social division and polarization. When such speech gets spread around, that is when our unity is threatened and when our unity gets dissolved, often with disastrous results.

There is another way in which these two types of speech are particularly revealing. When we either broadcast our pride in our own point of view or attack that of our opponents, it is one's self-concept that is being reflected. We are motivated by our concept of who we are, and it is the "me" and the "we" that give us a core set of meanings that define our world. And it is the sense of "me" that demands support and defends against rejection. That is where the emotions reside, a broader sense of our self-concept that we all carry around with us. As you will see in chapter 8, William James, the great American philosopher, says that we have as many selves as we do social groups with which we identify. When someone says, "I am a mother" or "I am an American" or "I am a Methodist," there is a strong melding of beliefs about the "I," the true "me" beneath it all, but there is also the sense of being part of a larger social entity, and that group identification is often as important as the individual "I." So we all identify ourselves both as an individual and as a group member, and this doubles the areas in which we invest our pride and emotional commitment. We become defensive and/or aggressive when we feel our worth is threatened by "the enemy." These distinctions between "radical supportive" and "radical attacking" neatly capture the dynamics of the complex and subtle ways in which we infuse emotions with our judgment processes. While the distinction between the individual self and the group self is an important one to keep in mind, we will also look at the principles of the dynamic ways in which various types of sayings and mottoes are in fact just surface manifestations of deeper-lying principles of the ways we perceive our world. In that sense, such phrases are not all that different from each other. They are just reflecting how our self-concepts become infused with bias, which can slant our judgments about the beliefs and behaviors of other people.

Social divisiveness has its destructive companions: prejudice, discrimination, aggression, and hate, all of which are part of human history. But at the opposite pole of the emotional continuum is excessive pride, blind devotion to a cause, in-group favoritism, and all-consuming partisanship. Both forms share a common psychological dynamic: narrow-mindedness and a failure to give all points of view fair consideration. Both forms of such emotional extremism are harmful to a unified society, and they have virtually eliminated the middle ground in our social discourse.

This is a book about the social psychology of radicalism. It is a review of research on fundamental *psychological* principles of the way the human mind obtains and processes information it receives from its environment, and the particular *social environment* in which it functions. The mind/emotion connection lies at the heart of radical hearing, and this will be given extensive coverage. There is hard scientific evidence on what causes us to treat each other so badly, yet that evidence is unknown both to our citizenry and to our social, political, and cultural leaders. The purpose of this book is to bring to public awareness the evidence that social researchers have discovered about the mental forces that are driving us apart

Wouldn't life be fine if we could all just get along with each other? If we all had the same tastes, the same beliefs, the same attitudes and opinions, the same goals—then we would have universal peace and could better focus our efforts on solving our earthly problems. At least, that is the dream of many. But it is most likely a pipe dream. Human history is one of interpersonal differences, of hard-core, nonnegotiable, intractable differences, which become so divisive that destruction of "the enemy" seems to be the only way to deal with our issues.

Unfortunately, there are so many ways to think of someone as your enemy: in terms of religion, politics, social class, language . . . the list of possible dividers is nearly endless. While this is unfortunate, it is important to understand that these feelings are entirely natural outcomes of the way our minds work. There is nothing abnormal about our social divisiveness, and that makes it imperative that we do something about it. The final chapter of this book discusses just how hard it will be to even begin to get started on restoring our unity.

A personal story will give you the essence of what this book is about. When I was an undergraduate and then a graduate student at the University of Oklahoma, my teacher and mentor was Dr. Muzafer Sherif, a truly brilliant social psychologist who made numerous foundational contributions in the social sciences. Under his guidance, I studied the effect of hot-emotions judgment processes, an area of research he pioneered.

At the time, the state of Oklahoma was under federal court order
to realign its voting districts to eliminate gross underrepresenta-
tion of the state's rapidly growing urban districts and domination by
thinly populated rural areas. You just cannot imagine the distress of
the rural districts at seeing their power diluted because of "federal
interference" (sound familiar?) and the anger among the urbanites
at having to fight for their rights.

With my testing materials, I traveled around the state, into this
boiling political cauldron, recruiting people who were either moderates, "strong pros," or "strong cons" on the issue. The theory and
methodological details of my study are discussed in chapter 6, so
here I will describe just the key components that taught me a lot
about humans and their emotions.

The task of the participants was to read and make a judgment
about the degree of opinion being represented by a set of statements
about the issue (the key method in this type of research). I developed a set of sixty one-sentence statements to cover the full range of
pro-to-con stances on the issue of the realignment of voting districts.
I had no money to pay the participants for their time (each volunteer
took about twenty minutes to rate the list of statements), so I had to
appeal to their civic sense of responsibility. I got an extremely high
rate of acceptance and surprisingly good data.

But going beyond my data for a moment, there are some aspects
of this experience that say a lot about where we are in this country. I
can present these aspects in the form of two "lessons."

Lesson 1. In retrospect, I am amazed that people were so helpful
and willing to take time out of their daily tasks to answer my questions. People were concerned, they were attentive, and they went out
of their way to be helpful to me, a stranger. It is an encouraging sign
when altruism is so easily elicited. Society needs bonding, and there
is a near-universal tendency among most people to be helpful and
supportive in their social relationships, even with a stranger. That
says a lot about keeping our social unity strong. But unfortunately I
also learned a second lesson.

Lesson 2. Obviously, people had to read the reapportionment statements in order to make a judgment about them. When they got to the statements they hated, here arose the anger, the upset, the red face. Their emotion immediately generalized beyond the judgment task. They got hostile about the entire project and several got so angry at me personally that I felt I had to leave as quickly as I could. So I did. Nice, friendly, helpful people can, in an instant, take on the intolerant, hostile, rejecting mentality we see these days in our divided, polarized society. It is truly bad news to think that we may be stuck with this kind of thinking forever.

There is one more angle to this problem that complicates things. To skip ahead to some actual results of studies on emotional biases (chapter 6), research has shown that we perceive our opponents to be biased in their thinking and unfair in what they do, and that they have poor arguments and are not telling the truth. When we are emotionally involved, we judge them as not having any credibility because we denigrate the very grounds of their opinions and beliefs. No wonder we need not listen to them! On the other hand, we are quite sure that we ourselves are fair and unbiased in our personal beliefs and attitudes, that we have good arguments and logic on our side, and that, of course, we feel that we always tell the truth. We are always on the side of the angels. So, naturally, we do not think of ourselves as "the problem"; it is those other people who are wrong about things. They deserved to be blamed.

There is an obvious trap in that logic. Following this way of thinking, those "other people" have the same self-justifying judgments about their perceptions, and they likely feel that they have fully valid reasons for disliking us because what we believe is unfair, biased, not true, and so on. So we end up with a society of people with mutual feelings of dislike, all of whom are equally self-justified and completely convinced that they are the correct ones. Given this standoff, why should you even *care* about what the other person thinks about you? After all, if they are not telling the truth, and they are biased and unfair in their beliefs, why should you try to get along with them? Or they with you? What kind of civic discourse can we expect when people perceive each other this way? Where can this lead? And is there anything that can be done about this locked-in social disaster? Right now, because of the very nature of the people and processes involved, tragedy is bound to occur. That is one powerful reason why human history is so filled with eliminationist thinking and action.

We need to find a way to get out of the circle. The scientific findings presented in this book first diagnose the problem and then propose techniques to show us a way out of our current discontent. I will discuss many living examples of how our divisiveness is harming our public discourse. Let me start with one recent example. As of 2012, the United States Congress and the executive branch have concluded, at least temporarily, an extremely intense and divisive debate over the budget of the government. Characterized by rancor, blaming, intransigence, and political "point making," a budget resolution was finally achieved with little or no satisfaction on either side. The word *side* is important here: Congress is, as usual, split along the lines of the two dominant political parties, Democrats and Republicans, and, as usual, differences of policies have become entrenched in deep-rooted, unalterable policies to be defended at all costs. As a result of the bickering, credit rating agencies have downgraded the US government's ratings for the first time in the history of the country. Political rancor was explicitly included as one major factor in the downgrading. Perhaps even worse, a so-called bipartisan supercommittee given total authority to resolve all budget differences eventually failed and went home with no compromises at all.

Why has this happened? Why has partisan rancor and aggressiveness become raised to such an intense level that the overall welfare of the country has become threatened? Where are we to look to find a reason for this potentially disastrous outcome? Once we understand the causes, then we have a good chance of doing something about it. It is the great challenge of our times: how to pull back from divisiveness and create a stronger sense of our social unity.

ONE SOURCE OF THE PROBLEM

Among all the rampant blaming and recriminations flying about, one key component of our discontent has not been publically discussed, at least not as far as I can determine. As I argue in this book, it is in the *very way that the human mind works* that the damaging polarization and divisiveness in our society have their poisonous origins. Dislike, discrimination, and denigration of others are common tools our minds use to handle "differentness." The key issue is how our perceptions and interpretations of our world get slanted and biased by our attitudes and emotions when we deal with other people and their beliefs and values.

Psychological science shows that our thoughts and interactions with others are not always neutral, cool, rational, deliberative, and, unfortunately, cooperative. In fact, our mind's perceptual and inter-pretational processes are highly subject to biases, slants, and distortions. These automatically color our relationships with others, who, in turn, experience the same biases, slants, and distortions. But where do these come from? This book proposes that in the public sphere, there are radical or extremist voices pushing for denigration and rejection of others whose beliefs they do not like. They push their own extremist agendas and attack their opponents' beliefs and values. The problem is, of course, that we are all "opponents" to someone else. Under this condition of hate speech, people sort themselves into opposing camps, with both sides feeling justified in engaging in heated rhetoric, in rejection, and especially, in moving away from the moderate middle out to the extreme ends of the con-tinuum. How does this circular system of destruction operate?

Fanned by inflammatory extremist speech of leading political, religious, and public media figures—who are often paid huge sums to peddle their wares of extremism—we find ourselves divided along numerous political, religious, and social fault lines. In this swirling vortex of discontent, emotions popularized by dominating media figures have come to dominate our reasoning. Worse, moderate voices that choose the path of accommodation and unity are not being heard. This loss of "the middle way" is why it is so important to understand the book's subtitle—How Emotions Warp What We Hear. Now the first half of the title of this book can be explained. I use the words "radical distortion" to explain the cognitive dynamics underlying radical speech and radical hearing. On any personal or social issue, there are many ways of thinking about it. The world is filled with alternatives, and we need to be flexible and thoughtfully engaged to meld the best of all of them. But radical speech tends to be unidimensional, to take just one course of thinking and while rejecting all others. The "distortion" comes in when numerous alternatives are not considered or, even worse, when all other alternatives are rejected. It is not so much that radical thinking is "wrong" as it is that it ignores or actively rejects often useful alternatives. Radical speakers and radical hearers have staked out one side of the issue, the good side (which of course is theirs), and they provide only positive information about their side and negative information about any alternative side. But by proclaiming only one side to be the true and correct side, and all other points of view to be wrong or dangerous, they are distorting the issue. With radical distortion, you end up with excessive certitude, rigidity, and closed mindedness.

This is not to say that our particular society at this particular time is somehow a special case demonstrating these polarizing tendencies. There have always been such divisive people, and they are not going to go away. But their voices will be lost to history, and they will have no effect *if people do not listen to them*. With no audience, there is no divisive effect. So if we are to create a society in which voices of moderation can be heard, then we must turn our attention to the *effects* of this "radical speech" that is poisoning our public discourse. We must turn our attention to the *audience*. When people come to endorse and accept extremist speech as their own, they are engaging in what I call "radical hearing." By this I refer to the complex psychological process of people who listen to and then accept radical speech, to people who actually *endorse* it. When they adopt it as their own, a complex process of biasing of their judgment processes becomes engaged. And it happens to all of us. To paraphrase the classic line of the cartoon character Pogo, "The enemy is us."

There are reasons why these divisions arise and have their enduring effects. The reasons have been the subject of intense investigation by psychologists for over half a century, and a great deal is now understood about how these processes operate within the human mind. Unfortunately, the general public is almost completely unaware of this body of research. But the divisiveness and polarization are occurring in the public domain, not in the research laboratories, so it is time to bring this research out to the public, where the knowledge can be shared and used to improve the situation.

THE SCIENCE OF INFORMATION SEARCH AND RETRIEVAL

The assumption that human beings are rational, clear-thinking, and calculating creatures has dominated philosophy and science for centuries. Indeed, the science of economics early on adopted the "rational man" model of economic behavior. Not everyone was convinced of this view, however. In other areas of thought, it has been posited that we are creatures of our emotions. This clash of paradigms is now coming to be resolved by discoveries that there are major ways in which bias and "illogic" actually dominate our thinking and decision making. This new wave of looking at our thinking had its birth in the pioneering work of Amos Tversky and Daniel Kahneman in their classic work *Judgment under Uncertainty*.[6] This book had such an immediate and powerful impact that Kahneman was awarded the Nobel Memorial Prize in Economic Sciences in 2002. Journalist Malcolm Gladwell brought this research to the public's attention in his bestselling book *Blink: The Power of Thinking without Thinking*,[7] and Kahneman has brought the field up to date in his recent book *Thinking, Fast and Slow*.[8]

In this now-classic line of research, Tversky and Kahneman presented empirical evidence from studies of reasoning and decision making showing that, among a wide range of conditions, human reasoning was basically flawed. When we need to consider all alternatives and weigh all the information, we very much underuse the available information and fall back on mental shortcuts. These "heuristics" (problem-solving strategies) are mental mechanisms that allow us to make quick decisions and to reduce our information search and cognitive-processing demands to a minimum. For example, we do not calculate statistical probabilities very well, so we tend to misjudge the role of luck in our outcomes. If we have to process information under time pressure, we grab the first thing that comes to mind. We tend to sell a winning stock too quickly and keep holding on to a losing stock. We overrate the degree to which other people agree with us. Overall, it is not that humans are irrational; it is that we employ rational-thinking processes that are inadequately based, that are subject to wrong assumptions about the world, and that are slanted toward efficiency and quickness in reasoning rather than toward adequacy and comprehensiveness. In the neat description by Susan Fiske and Shelley Taylor, "We may be fast, but we aren't very good."[9]

From the perspective of this book, there is one critical issue that has not been studied very thoroughly in this research tradition. The research has not extended to hot-button, high-emotion issues such as are involved in radical speech and radical hearing. Decision studies tend to be performed experimentally in psychology and economics research laboratories rather than having investigators searching out and studying the reasoning processes and heuristics among angry, attacking radical hearers. It is this realm—the real world of hot-button emotions and intergroup frictions—in which our divisiveness and polarization are based. The cognitive heuristics approach is indeed a valuable one when it comes to studying how our reasoning and decision making are biased by various cognitive heuristic processing, so considering emotion-based biased reasoning, we can get a fuller picture of the difficulties we are going to face if we want to find some way to reunite people and reduce our divisions.

Psychological science tells us about human perception processes, the thinking and decision-making processes that motivate human social interactions, but it must also account for the mainsprings of our emotions and our struggles to achieve what we want, to achieve our desires and goals. Sometimes this involves attacking our enemy. There are specific, distinctive characteristics of those processes that arise when radical hearing gets engaged, which occurs when a person's thinking and decision-making processes become biased by hot-button emotions. Research (which I will discuss in later chapters) shows that emotions have the effect of reducing our ability to make careful, logical distinctions about what we are hearing. This results in, literally, simple-minded, two-category, black-and-white thinking. Voices of moderation are simply not heard when such emotion-based biases get activated in radical hearing.

Much of this pioneering research was begun by careful analysis of how thinking and deciding operates for the individual. That is an individual-based kind of analysis. But that is only one part of the picture. Research has extended beyond the principles of our thinking processes into the social realm. Humans live out their lives in social contexts, and it is there that the effects of radical hearing get magnified by social forces in the person's environment. This research on the social psychology of intergroup relations shows that discrimination, prejudice, and hostilities are an inherent part of our social relationships. In reviewing this research, I will devote a good deal of discussion to one of the most amazing experiments ever conducted in the social sciences. The Robbers Cave study (discussed in detail in chapter 8) involved two groups of young boys at a summer camp who, through the mere act of engaging in a sports contest for desirable prizes, spiraled downward into near war, a situation similar to that described by William Golding in his book *Lord of the Flies*.[10] Every fiber of these boys was emotionally committed to warring against their "enemies," boys just like themselves responding to the same situational dynamics.

ORGANIZATION OF THIS BOOK

A medical analogy will give you an idea of how this book is structured. First, I provide a *description* of the problem of radical hearing. Next, I give a detailed *diagnosis* of what is causing the problem, and I discuss a method of *treatment* of the problem. Finally, I explore fundamental cognitive and emotional reasons why radical hearing is going to be difficult to eliminate from our civic discourse. Ultimately, it is up to the individual reader, and the citizenry, to decide if they wish to continue on with the divided, polarized society that currently confronts us.

To provide more detail, chapter 1 begins with numerous examples of what might be called "hate speech," although that harsh term misses some distinctions that I will show to be important as beginning points. The chapter explains several types of radical speech and why only one type, *radical-attacking speech*, is the critical factor to creating radical hearing. Chapters 2 and 3 review basic scientific research on human judgment processes, which are then extended to the measurement of attitudes and beliefs. This advancement created a revolution in revealing how hot-button issues elicit biases and distortions in our personal judgment scales. Chapters 4, 5, and 6 discuss numerous studies showing how the same basic principles of judgment occur in many different types of social, political, and religious beliefs. The key finding is that extremists on either side of a hot-button topic behave identically: Biased speakers and hearers are not opposite each other; they are identical in the types of biases and distortions in their judgments compared to moderates who are not ego-involved. Research consistently shows that it is not *where* one stands on an issue; it is how *emotionally biased* one is regarding that issue.

Chapter 7 summarizes the first six chapters of the book and then provides a list of the main principles that characterize radical hearing in our everyday lives. This includes a checklist of these characteristics so that the reader can get the essence of how radical hearing can be identified in anyone, including themselves.

Chapter 8 moves to the social level of intergroup relations, showing how they contain the seeds of polarization. This polarization begins at the most basic level of social interaction, when people perceive someone else negatively by virtue of their simply being "different." In-group/out-group discrimination and even hostilities are based on simple distinctions of differentness, but competition for resources engages and then enhances the judgmental biases presented in the previous chapters, and we see formerly happy, cooperative, "normal" American boys engaged in a war against each other when their emotional involvement becomes extreme. This is radical hearing carried out to its logical consequences.

In chapter 9, I show how the principles of radical hearing revealed by psychological research can be turned on their side and used to reduce or eliminate our radical hearing and its divisiveness. The material here reviews the previous research but inverts it by showing how understanding those principles opens up new pathways for reforming our own personal ways of thinking. Each individual can change their social relationships in ways that can reduce or eliminate the damaging effects of radical hearing. If we apply these principles as I recommend, then maybe voices of moderation can get the fair hearing they deserve. However, it may be that people will not take the suggestions in chapter 9 to heart, and they might not make any attempts to change their radical hearing.

The final chapter presents logical arguments that explain why people may choose to ignore my suggestions and not change their patterns of radical hearing. I see two sources responsible for a resistance to change: *cognitive* (people will not change because, cognitively, they cannot change) and *emotional* (they will not change because they do not want to change). A call for overcoming these two sources is the essence of the final chapter of the book.

A DISCLAIMER

There are a lot of emotionally charged topics in this book. There is a good chance that the reader will find some of the statements of beliefs personally touchy, if not upsetting. I have deliberately tried *not* to choose sides on any hot-button issues. There has been no attempt to make anyone look bad or look good. I do not say that anybody is right or wrong in their beliefs. But I do say, with real data from really emotional people, that highly committed individuals are biased in their judgment processes and are therefore very likely to threaten our social unity. Because of that bias, the voices of moderate, unbiased people are not being heard. There is only one motivating reason behind this book: to show fairly and objectively how radical hearing occurs, what effects it has, and how the principles underlying it give us clear ways to eliminate it from our poisoned public discourse. It is up to all of us.

Now is a critical time to bring the powerful insights from this psychological research out of the realm of technical, professional social science and into the general public domain. My intent is to raise public consciousness of the dangers of radical hearing. I believe that we now have an excellent opportunity to understand its implications for getting ourselves out of our current loop of divisive public discourse.

CHAPTER 1
DELIBERATE DIVISIVENESS

Under ordinary circumstances, our social relations, our bonds with our family, our friends, our community, even our ties to our nation should be our most precious national resources and should be treated accordingly. Our connectedness with our society should be a wellspring of our resilience as we try to adapt to our fast-changing and challenging future. But these are not ordinary circumstances, and our unity is under attack. There are people in our midst who are intent on destroying it, who deliberately want to divide us from each other. And they are succeeding in significant ways. This is an amazing and depressing phenomenon. It is amazing and depressing because some of those people are being paid millions of dollars to do this. They have been raised to the exalted status of media stars. With their radical and polarizing speech, they are the loudest voices of our times. They are so successful that voices of moderation are being drowned out.

But this is not "news." Our national unity perpetually seems to be a fragile thing, threatened when events unleash our emotions and make us question our relationships with each other. A recent tragedy in my sister city of Tucson, Arizona (I live in Tempe), highlights how tenuous our unity truly is. On a beautiful Arizona morning, Saturday, January 8, 2011, our US representative from Arizona's Eighth District, third-term congresswoman Gabrielle Giffords, was holding an open "Congress on Your Corner" public meeting with her constituents in a Safeway® parking lot when a man, later identified as Jared Loughner, opened fire with a handgun. Representative Giffords was seriously wounded, six people died, and thirteen others were injured. Giffords survived the initial injuries and of this writing is reported to be showing excellent progress in rehabilitation.

This premeditated attack unleashed a firestorm of controversy over Loughner's motives, with speculation initially centering on his political leanings. Right after the shooting, people decried the high level of divisiveness and rancor in our public media. Giffords was a Democrat and had just come off a strong, challenging midterm election against a conservative Republican. In fact, Giffords's own office had been vandalized after she participated in a rancorous debate over healthcare reform. Speculation then turned to the status of Loughner's mental health. At this time, there have been no official statements on this subject, and no trial has been held to clarify the matter.

What is interesting from my perspective is how the national debate over the event has evolved. I see post-tragedy developments as falling into two related categories: (1) Many commentators quickly noted the presence of vitriol and divisiveness in our public media that might have stimulated violent thoughts in the gunman, so there was a reaction against media incitement, and (2) People said they would take concrete actions to move toward more accommodation and unity. Let me give some examples of both of these developments since they foreshadow many of the issues I want to discuss further.

Among the media outlets commenting on event, Tucson's *Arizona Daily Star* editorialized on the day after the shooting: "The immediate reaction of some has been to point to the poisonous atmosphere that has engulfed Arizona and the nation. Gun imagery, talking of 'targeting' elected officials and taking out political opponents has become pervasive. The bitter 2010 election turned up the volume. Demonizing people who have different opinions makes for easy punditry and cheap entertainment. It has to stop. . . . It shouldn't take a massacre for us to talk to each other instead of only about each other."[1]

In addition, Dr. Paul Krugman, Nobel Prize–winning economist and columnist for the *New York Times*, sought to have the nation stop what he called "eliminationist rhetoric." In his January 9 article, he said, "The point is that there's room in a democracy for people who ridicule and denounce those who disagree with them; there isn't any place for eliminationist rhetoric, for suggestions that those on the other side of a debate must be removed from that debate by whatever means necessary. And it's the saturation of our political discourse— and especially our airwaves—with eliminationist rhetoric that lies behind the rising tide of violence."[2]

There is good evidence from the science of attitudes and emotions that there are deep-seated mental tendencies for people to reject and eliminate the ideas of people with whom they disagree. And regarding the *Arizona Daily Star* editorial, I am afraid that when the editor said, "It has to stop," that clarion call simplified what is a deeply difficult thing to do, as I will show. However, in the next-to-last chapter of this book, after all the evidence is in, I will provide evidence-based suggestions as to how we might go about changing our judgment processes and our ways of approaching intergroup differences. It might not happen as I say in my final chapter, and, if it does not come about, it will be for understandable reasons that are provided in the following chapters.

Now to my second category of post-tragedy responses. In the public furor over the Tucson incident, a number of prominent people actually started doing something to turn down the heat. Perhaps the most significant action, from a national perspective, was that congressional leaders themselves took action to reduce the inflammatory rhetoric and to increase the civility of our discourse. Interviewed by the media, a number of officials said that they intended to work more closely with the members of the opposition political party in an attempt to be more bipartisan. In fact, two leading senators at the opposite ends of the political spectrum, Charles Schumer of New York and Tom Coburn of Oklahoma, agreed to sit together to hear the upcoming State of the Union address by President Barack Obama. By tradition, members of the two major parties sit separately during the speech—as amazing as that may seem from a psychological perspective. I will present research in chapter 8 that shows how exactly *wrong* separation like this is if one wants to enhance intergroup cooperation rather than contention.

Interestingly, President Obama himself made reference to this remarkable turnaround. In his 2011 State of the Union address, he said, "What comes of this moment is up to us. What comes of this moment will be determined not by whether we can sit together tonight, but whether we can work together tomorrow. . . . We will move forward together, or not at all—for the challenges we face are bigger than party, and bigger than politics."[3]

A note of caution is always appropriate, especially when dealing with politics. On May 22, a mere four and a half months after Giffords was shot, two journalists from McClatchy Newspapers, David Lightman and William Douglas, reviewed the current political scene in Washington. Their article "Compromise Tough in D.C." pointed to two major factors that make compromise difficult: "Yet changes in the political culture are clearly adding great pressure, triggered by interdependent forces: an inescapable news media and increasing polarized views. Together they challenge congressional leaders' ability to broker the compromise essential to successful democratic government."[4]

One more development signals the post-tragedy awareness of the dangers of our current divisiveness. The University of Arizona, which is in Gabrielle Giffords's electoral district, announced on February 21, 2011, the formation of the National Institute for Civil Discourse. This nonpartisan center is devoted to research, education, and policy formulation to enhance civility in public discourse. On its board of directors are former presidents Bill Clinton and George H. W. Bush, and former Supreme Court justice Sandra Day O'Connor (from Arizona), along with many other national figures well versed in national politics.

These are encouraging developments toward enhancing our national unity and countering the efforts of public figures who are making big bucks to divide us. But our public conversation about extremism would be greatly improved if we would put our debate on a foundation of reliable, grounded, hard-core scientific evidence. This evidence would have to reveal what happens to the human mind when it gets poisoned by the emotions of anger and hate. Although it does not get mentioned in public debate, this anger is invariably accompanied by corollary side effects, such as a sense of superiority, of self-pride, of inflexible certainty about being in the right, and of rejection of moderate points of view. The motto "My way or the highway" characterizes much of this rhetoric.

Actually, this type of social polarization has received considerable research attention lately. Political scientists have been able to measure such quantitative variables as political party registration and voting pattern. They then relate those measures to other variables, such as demographic trends and national opinion polling results. Robin Stryker of the National Institute for Civil Discourse summarized research studying the partisanship of the leaders of our national political parties and voter polling results. She showed that there is good evidence that voters' opinions do not show as much polarization as does the party leadership. "Institutional change in the American political system has incentivized party candidates, leaders and office holders to stake out more, rather than less, extreme positions . . . there still may be cause for concern to the extent that polarization is accompanied with greater incivility in political discourse."[5]

Even more revealing, these researchers have been attempting to answer a sort of chicken and egg problem: Has party leadership been the source of the polarization, or have the voters themselves become more extreme in their partisanship, with leaders simply reflecting that in their party platforms? The answer to these questions is a matter of debate because it is difficult to establish precise characteristics of polarization within the voting public itself, whereas assessing polarization among the leadership is a more clear-cut matter. Nevertheless, summing up the results of the available studies, Stryker has been able to conclude that "elite party polarization and mass polarization now feed on each other, but evidence suggests that partisan activists were the original instigators of this reciprocal polarization dynamic."[6]

This is an important conclusion. It points to the role that prominent, highly publicized national figures have an impact on forming people's attitudes and beliefs about significant political issues and, by extension, religious and social policy issues as well. If we want to work against our current divisiveness and polarization, we have to focus on the ways that partisan and extremist speech affect the public at large.

So we need to ask the question, Can something be done about this state of affairs? If we are to have any hope of social unity, there are two major issues to consider. First, we have to understand it. With a clear understanding of what is happening, we then have a chance of finding the best way to eliminate the problem. If reducing the divisiveness and restoring our national sense of unity is our most important public goal—and I believe that it should be—then the second issue to consider is, can we then figure out how to achieve it?

In my opinion, and based on the best scientific evidence, the answer to both of these questions is a resounding yes. Yes, we do know a great deal about this type of public speech, and we know a great deal about its effects on people. And to answer the second question, yes, we can figure out what to do about it. I will provide a set of principled suggestions at the end of this book that will show us the best ways to accomplish this. The critical consideration, however, is that psychological research is showing us that it will be very difficult for us to "get along." There are strong cognitive and social forces for keeping us separate.

I have taught this information to university undergraduate and graduate students for many years, and I will present some of my own research findings on these topics later in this book. But while the psychology of judgment and decision making in high-emotion, hot-button issues has been a well-researched topic in psychological science, the research can only have benefits to us all if the public knows of it and adopts suggestions along the lines of those I propose for improving our public discourse. I suspect that even "radical speakers" (my term) who engage in divisive speech do not have any background knowledge in this type of work. I want to encourage a public dialogue about where we are in our current civic discourse. The information in this book is a solid starting point for that dialogue and, I hope, for action.

To answer the first question—can something be done about this state of affairs?—this book presents some powerful concepts from psychological research on how this divisive, polarizing speech has its effects. That research reveals the ways in which the human mind gets twisted and distorted by the hostile, aggressive emotions that arise from radical, extremist speech. These effects operate at the level of the individual's thinking, judgment, and decision-making processes. However, there are also sources of friction that lay outside the realm of the person's mind; they reside in our social relations, in our identifying ourselves with social groups—with "us" and "them." This kind of divisiveness also affects our mental processing. So it is the combination of the biasing of our individual mental processing and our aggressive social relations where we find the core causes of our problems in civil discourse with each other.

As for solving this problem, surely we should be smart enough to use those very same principles to answer the second question, a question of applying our knowledge to our daily living. That's the hard one, particularly if it refers to tolerating people whose politics or religion we dislike. But I will show that we know what to do and that we can succeed if we have the individual and public will to do so—that we can act on what we know from understanding those principles.

REAL EXAMPLES OF REALLY RADICAL SPEECH

The immediate reason for our own polarization is obvious: popular, forceful public figures who denigrate and vilify their targets. These people are radicals and extremists, and they are often proud of it. You know them because they are vividly displayed in the public limelight. They are on the radio, the television, at conventions, in the pulpit; they write inflammatory books and articles. They are polarizers. Author and columnist John Avlon describes what these people do as "polarizing for profit."[7] With their black-and-white beliefs, they tolerate no deviance from the "true word," and anyone who is not for them is against them. Avlon has coined a useful phrase to describe the most aggressive of these people: "Hatriots." It is a term that captures their aggressiveness clothed in the language of patriotism.[8] Who are these people? As we shall see, there are plenty of examples of extremists on one side or another of many different issues—the political, religious, and social issues that divide us today.

Television commentator and author Rush Limbaugh, one of today's most popular public commentators, had this to say about Democrats: "We've always known that Democrats are antiwar, and we've always known that we can't really count on them when it comes to national defense. But we have finally seen with whom they will go to war: The American people who disagree with them."[9]

On the same topic, Limbaugh has said, "They are some of the meanest, most vile people in the country—the supporters of the Democrat Party and the Obama ticket. They are deranged, they are unhinged, and they are genuinely dangerous, but the media will only praise them as being 'activists' and 'involved.'"[10]

Another well-known public commentator and author, Ann Coulter, has similar feelings, but they are directed at liberals: "While the form of treachery varies slightly from case to case, liberals always manage to take the position that most undermines American security."[11]

On the other side of the political spectrum, Keith Olbermann, journalist and television commentator, made this observation about the Republican administration's response to the Hurricane Katrina disaster in New Orleans: "This is the Law and Order and Terror Government. It promised protection—or at least amelioration against all threats: conventional, radiological, or biological. It has just proved that it cannot save its citizens from a biological weapon called standing water."[12]

Even presidents engage in radical speech about their opponents. Commenting on the nature of conservatives, President Franklin Roosevelt, a Democrat, stated: "A conservative is a man with two perfectly good legs who, however, has never learned how to walk forward."[13]

These are bitter words, contemptuous of the opponent, and extremist. I wonder if the speaker could have made the same point without being so divisive. It is hard to imagine uniting our people when such speech dominates the public media. One reason for the destructiveness was pointed out in the nineteenth century by one of America's leading poets, James Russell Lowell: "Toward no crimes have men shown themselves so cold-bloodedly cruel as in punishing differences of belief."[14]

Another American literary icon, Ralph Waldo Emerson, was concerned about radicalism as part of the American character: "The spirit of our American radicalism is destructive and aimless; it is not loving; it has no ulterior and divine ends; but is destructive only out of hatred and selfishness."[15]

Our difficulty in having moderate, open-minded civil discourse with each other in these times reflects the effects of the ongoing cultural wars and campaigns of destructive divisiveness we are currently experiencing. Robert F. Kennedy, former US attorney general, once noted: "What is objectionable, what is dangerous, about extremists is not that they are extreme, but that they are intolerant. The evil is not what they say about their cause, but what they say about their opponents."[16]

It is not clear that things have changed very much since these early descriptions of our national character. The properties of some of the more vocal of these speakers are so sharply defined, so distinctive, that they deserve their own label, a term that places them in a special status. Such people meet the description of a *fanatic*. This term was perfectly defined by Winston Churchill, who has been quoted widely as defining it as a person who "can't change his mind and won't change the subject." Churchill was describing fanatics in the realm of politics, his own field. But the description characterizes religious debate, public-policy debate, family disputes, arguments about hot-button social issues, or just two individuals screaming at each other over some disagreement. Shouting matches are seldom constructive, but they are common. It is amazing how often people raise their voices and shout down each other. To find just one example of this type of behavior, I suggest that you go online and open the video website YouTube® and type in the search terms "Bill O'Reilly flips out on Barney Frank + banking crisis + mad screaming match" or "Bill O'Reilly vs. Barney Frank." These types of encounters are intense and scary.

Do these two people think that the other person is actually *hearing* them? Surely not! As we shall see, people do not "hear" when they are boiling with emotional involvement. I suspect that the average moderate person viewing this debate could not learn anything from it, but O'Reilly supporters will like what he says and will hate what Barney Frank says, and Barney Frank's supporters will like what he says and hate what O'Reilly says. It seems pretty obvious to me that shouting at someone is no way to get them to agree with you. But interestingly, psychologists now know why shouting will not work. There has always been hate speech in some form or another as far back as records show, and in many ways the same speech exists today. But what is new is that we have a much clearer understanding of the *psychological basis* of this type of speech. Psychological science has become a highly sophisticated field, and it has been applied to human (and animal) cognitive processes. That research has shown that our thinking about what we hear is very sensitive to emotions, and emotions basically shut down our judgment and deliberations about what we hear. How that happens is complicated, and I will discuss research that unlocks some of the complications. Knowing how those complications operate gives us pathways to finding out how to reduce the damaging effects that emotions have on our thinking processes.

Ordinary debate with such people almost never changes their minds, and they are not going to stop being extreme and polarizing.

So it seems clear that any chance for reducing the level of public hostility and paralyzed politics and religious conflict has to come at another level, the psychological level of the minds of people who hear and respond to radical speech.

There are two very potent characteristics of radical speech, and both have critical components that give them their destructive impact when people come to accept them as part of their own belief systems.

1. *Intense emotion.* Extremist speech is characterized by intense emotional words and thoughts that express two kinds of extreme emotions. On the one hand are hostility, aggression, and hate toward "the enemy." On the other side of the same coin, are patriotic pride, haughtiness, unquestioning devotion, and divinely inspired certitude. Middle-of-the-road emotions are not even needed in this mental set; they are not expressed so dramatically and cannot be heard.

2. *Cognitive simplicity.* This term refers to two-category thinking, black-and-white reasoning, with little or no consideration of moderate, more complex or more abstract reasoning. Small but important distinctions of meaning get lost, and quick and easy distinctions (such as "our side = good" and "their side = bad") dominate this type of thinking.

Some research presented in upcoming chapters will provide results whereby you can actually see the effects of such two-category thinking. There is a related aspect of this type of simplistic thinking. The joking phrase "Don't bother me with facts, my mind is made up" appropriately sums up in one idea what happens when the judging process breaks down. In the context of this book, though, it is not very funny.

The model of radical speech that I am following in this book has the direct implication that if you endorse someone's extremism and adopt their beliefs and attitudes as your own, then inexorably you will adopt the same intense emotions and cognitive simplicity that they have. It is a small step for people to label you as a "Hitlerite" if you endorse Hitler's speech. There are personal consequences of your endorsement of radical speech: you will experience a drastic shift toward simplicity and emotional extremism in your own judgment processes, and you may well become regarded by other people in the same way that they think about your role models. And even if there aren't consequences for you personally, society will be subjected to just one more unit of polarization and dysfunction when you put your extreme speech into practice.

TWO TYPES OF RADICAL SPEECH

You may have noted that up to this point I have used the term "hate speech" several times. Although that might appear to be the most obvious term for the examples of extremist speech I have presented, I feel it is too crude to pick up important distinctions. For one thing, not all extremist speech expresses hate; often, it expresses strong advocacy or enthusiasm for its topic. The term "radical speech" is more useful, which is why I have chosen it for this book. Looking carefully at the examples of radical speech actually shows that they have some important distinguishing properties. Those properties give us a better understanding of how that kind of speech has its effects. In fact, there are at least two general types of extremist speech. One might be called *radical-supporting*. In this type, the speaker is making extremist speech, but it is focused on saying radical but positive or favorable things about his or her own point of view, praising and claiming absolute truth on just one side of an issue (naturally, his or her "side"). This type of speech is still divisive, proclaiming that one's side is superior, but without specific aggressiveness or divisiveness about "the other side." The second type of radical speech can be called *radical-attacking*, and it is just what it sounds like: speech that is hostile and aggressive, attacking a person or beliefs on the "other side," which the speaker is deliberately trying to denigrate. This second category is perhaps the most destructive for society because it tries to drive a wedge between us. Clearly, these days, it is succeeding.

It seems that being a strong advocate for one particular point of view—let's say a religious belief, or party platform, or social issue—might be fairly common in public discourse and not particularly divisive. Many examples of this radical-supporting speech come readily to mind. For instance, we expect advertising firms to come up with strong, clear, and convincing advertisements for their particular products or services. We have come to expect our political candidates and religious leaders to praise their own viewpoints and to claim that they have the answers to our own problems if we will just believe what they say and vote for them. This type of touting is expected in newspaper, magazine, and television commercials. You can take or reject the message. We expect hype and extravagant praise for something the speaker is advocating, so such speech has no particularly destructive societal consequences. Here are some examples of "radical-supporting" speech.

Pat Buchanan, a candidate running for presidential office, said, "Our culture is superior. Our culture is superior because our religion is Christianity and that is the truth that makes men free."[17]

Britain's King George III, the main nemesis of the American revolutionaries and patriots, held firm to his birthright: "Born and educated in this country, I glory in the name of Briton."[18]

Teddy Roosevelt was a real booster for American well-being: "Americanism means the virtues of courage, honor, justice, sincerity, and hardihood—the virtues that made America."[19]

The second category of radical speech, radical-attacking, is more relevant to our current divisiveness and polarization. Speakers of this type have the explicit aim of dividing people into two groups, the good people and the bad people, and they do everything possible to attack the bad people. Here is Adolf Hitler, one of the greatest radical-attacking speakers, proclaiming his opinion of Jewish people:

> The internal expurgation of the Jewish spirit is not possible in any platonic way. For the Jewish spirit is the product of the Jewish

person. Unless we expel the Jewish people soon, they will have juda-ized our people within a very short time.

. . . the personification of the devil as the symbol of all evil assumes the living shape of the Jew.[20]

We have similar calls for divisiveness in our own time and closer to home. One well-known religious leader and prominent public figure, the Reverend Fred Phelps of Kansas, commented on the murder of a young gay man, Matt Shepard, "Not only is homosexuality a sin, but anyone who supports fags is just as guilty as they are: You are both worthy of death."[21]

Concerning religion, Phelps has said, "The Jews of Temple Beth Sholom are sinful, greedy, Hell-bound, money-grubbing sodomites; and they have dedicated their synagogue to be a gay and lesbian propaganda mill and recruiting depot, soliciting young people to sodomy."[22]

Other radical speech is a bit more indirect. One tactic is to attack an issue with which "the other side" is identified, making sure to denigrate it as much as possible. For instance, Henry Morris, director of the Institute for Creation Research and a strong advocate for Christianity, goes far beyond supporting his own religion when he said this about Charles Darwin's theory of human evolution: "Evolution is the root of atheism, of communism, Nazism, behaviorism, racism, economic imperialism, militarism, libertinism, anarchism, and all manner of anti-Christian systems of belief and practice."[23]

Pat Robertson, evangelical minister and television show host, had this to say about the national organization Planned Parenthood. "[Planned Parenthood] is teaching kids to fornicate, teaching people to have adultery, every kind of bestiality, homosexuality, lesbianism—everything that the Bible condemns."[24]

And about the women's rights movement, Robertson said, "The feminist agenda is not about equal rights for women. It is about a socialist, antifamily political movement that encourages women to leave their husbands, kill their children, practice witchcraft, destroy capitalism, and become lesbians."[25]

Other commentators have taken equally divisive stands against religion (as opposed to merely supporting their own point of view). Robert Ingersoll, a leading social commentator in the mid-1800s said about liberty and governance: "There can be little liberty on earth while men worship a tyrant in heaven."[26]

At about the same time, German philosopher Friedrich Nietzsche wrote, "After coming into contact with a religious man I always feel I must wash my hands."[27]

More recently, and more pertinent to the issues raised by Pat Robertson, paleontologist Stephen J. Gould said: "The fundamentalists, by 'knowing' the answers before they start (examining evolution), and then forcing nature into the straitjacket of their discredited preconceptions, lie outside the domain of science—or of any honest intellectual inquiry."[28]

British biologist and author Richard Dawkins stated in an interview, "Evolution should be one of the first things you learn at school . . . and what do they [children] get instead? Sacred hearts and incense. Shallow, empty religion."[29]

The two categories of speech are so common in our everyday discourse that we may tend to overlook the major differences between them. For someone to be *radically supporting* a particular point of view says a lot about them (and their supporters, of course), but it does not necessarily involve any direct divisiveness or rejection of other people. But when the speech turns to *radical-attacking*, then it has the ability to poison our thinking about "the other" or "the enemy." Radical-supporting speech might be expected from anyone who has a love of something, elevated self-esteem, and pride in their accomplishments. It is a natural extension of pursuing and achieving desired goals. Radical-supporting speech is interesting in its own right, and it underpins a major industry: advertising. But if you do not want the product, you can just ignore the hype. Get up off the couch and go to the fridge when the ad comes on.

But radical-attacking speech is an entirely different matter. I provide so many examples of it because it is the main fuel for our current social divisions. If some extremist attacks your values, that raises your sense of threat and self-defense, and some retaliation is demanded. I call this "psychological reactance" in the next chapter. A cycle of attack-response-counterattack is engaged, and the air gets poisoned with hostility. This is the key problem with radical-attack speech: it can become endless, and time that could be better spent on more productive pursuits gets eaten up with hate. Because of the rise of cable television and social media (blogs, YouTube, Facebook®, Twitter®), radical speech has many more avenues than in past years. It can aggravate an already serious social problem. It unleashes aggressive forces intended to harm its target; in it lurks the danger for our social unity and the safety and security of the bonds that hold us together.

FROM SPEECH TO HEARING

Although radical-attacking speech is the clear public cause of our divisions and polarization tendencies, it is only half of the equation. If people did not actually hear that speech, if they would ignore it or just let it go past them, and then it would *have no effect.* Our social divisiveness and polarization cannot gain traction if radical-attacking speech is not seriously listened to or believed by someone. Even more than that, though, to be effective in polarizing people, the speech not only has to be heard; it has to be *endorsed* by the hearer; it has to be adopted and accepted internally. Such a process gives us a special set of terms to make clearer the sources of our divisiveness. Here are the terms, which I use throughout this book:

> *Radical speech.* 1. Departing markedly from the usual or customary; extreme. 2. Favoring or effecting fundamental or revolutionary changes in current practices, conditions, or institutions.

Radical hearing. To listen to radical speech and to judge it as acceptable to the self; to endorse radical speech as one's own, to make radical speech as part of one's self-identity.

By considering the entire loop from speaker to hearer, we get a fuller picture of where polarization has taken hold of the public discourse. But that picture is complex and needs to be separated into its key components. When we understand those components, then we will be able to explain the consequences of radical hearing. Fortunately, research has uncovered a complex web of subtle processes in the thinking of people who have become radical hearers. The endorsement process itself is a rather complex intertwining of several distinct psychological steps the mind takes when dealing with external events such as exposure to speech. Research on these steps gives us valuable insights into how it is that people become so committed and inflexible in their beliefs, so I devote special attention to this process in chapter 2. By getting a better understanding of these processes, we can see how it is that polarized thinking has come to dominate our public discourse. It has become a social problem, but it is really a question of human psychology. This is where human judgment and decision-making processes become engaged, reflecting basic principles of how we perceive and understand our world. They also show how we *mis*perceive the world, the bias inherent in radical hearing.

ISN'T MODERATION THE ANSWER?

The common-sense approach to dividing and polarizing speech is for people to reject it and to endorse moderate, cool opinions. Wouldn't we be better off if everyone simply rejected radical speech and chose the path of moderation? Common sense might suggest this approach, but our current problems of disunity are very complex, and I think that common sense will fail us here. As we review what we know of human judgment, it turns out that moderation is not such a simple goal. In fact, even moderation is controversial and can become yet another source of divisiveness and disagreement. Returning to our trusty Internet search again, here are some revealing quotations about moderation which are widely attributed to the persons named:

> "Never go to excess, but let moderation be your guide." Cicero, Roman philosopher and orator.

However, moderation is not necessarily the answer. There are plenty of criticisms about being a moderate:

> "Moderation in temper is always a virtue, but moderation in principle is always a vice." Thomas Paine, author of *Common Sense* and leader in the American Revolution.

> "When the sword is once drawn, the passions of men observe no bounds of moderation." Alexander Hamilton, leader in the American Revolution.

> "We know what happens to people who stay in the middle of the road. They get run down." Aneurin Bevan, Welsh Labor Party leader.

> "And let me remind you also that moderation in the pursuit of justice is no virtue." Barry Goldwater, accepting the Republican presidential nomination, 1964.

> "Moderation? It's mediocrity, fear, and confusion in disguise. . . . It's the devil's dilemma. It's the wobbling compromise that makes no one happy. Moderation is for the bland, the apologetic, for the fence-sitters of the world afraid to take a stand." Dan Millman, author of *Way of the Peaceful Warrior.*

Obviously, these quotations do not provide a ringing endorsement of moderation. Apparently, it can even be dangerous to be a moderate;

after all, who wants to "get run down"? Being a moderate can get you labeled with a social stigma, as a blank, as apologetic, and as a fence-sitter. In our current polarized political, religious, and social climate, it seems that the most radical people have pushed moderate voices from the public stage. Indeed, as I write this book, the Republican Party is finding its major moderate leaders being voted out by more extreme partisans, many of whom label themselves members of the Tea Party. If there is any open conflict between the voices of radical speech and voices of moderation, it seems that right now moderation is not doing very well. In fact, research shows us that because of the ways that emotions poison our thinking processes, moderation simply *cannot* be heard. And this book's subtitle, "How Emotions Warp What We Hear," describes precisely what the research data are telling us. If we give in to our emotions, we will have a nation in which in black-and-white, two-category thinking dominates public discussion. Given the complex world in which we live, I hope that we can avoid conditions in which our thinking gets shrunk down to cognitive and emotional simplicity. That is why, in the upcoming chapters, I systematically review what research tells us about communication processes when speech gets radical and when people start engaging in radical hearing. The key to this has been uncovered by research psychologists using sophisticated and especially clever ways of revealing the dynamics and principles underlying why it is that "voices of moderation can't be heard."

The upcoming chapters lay the foundation for presenting that research, and they follow a consistent theme: reviewing the concepts and methods of research studies of emotions and human decision and judgment. The methods and the displays of results (data) from these studies may seem unfamiliar at first, but the unique feature of this body of research is that the methods reflect *exactly* how the mind is processing. When people make judgments about what a radical speaker is saying, that is exactly what the method is assessing, and the displays of the data resulting from these studies reflect exactly what people do when they react to that speaker. There are some technical terms, but they will be quite clear and meaningful as the discussion goes along. Finally, there is a distinct sequence of topics in this book: from simple judgment tasks to group conflict and war . . . they are all reflections of a sequence of processes described systematically. If we understand that sequence, then perhaps we can find a way to back out of our current social discontent and build a better life for everyone.

CHAPTER 2
THE PSYCHOLOGY OF BECOMING COMMITTED

In spite of all the examples of hateful talk I gave in chapter 1, we humans nevertheless have the capacity to be cool, rational, thinking, and calculating organisms. We are not always so hot-tempered and quick to reject others; at least, that is what we tell ourselves. We are not always dominated by our passions, and we would not do as good a job of getting along in life as we do if we were always so emotional about things. But when our emotions get aroused, our passions can lead us to make bad decisions, sometimes fatal ones. If you get cut off in traffic, you can be cool and logical and figure out how to handle the situation, or you can let your emotions take over and "lose it." We call such behavior "road rage," and sometimes it feels good to blow off our anger and frustration. In such a situation, events happen so quickly that it is not easy to control yourself. But losing your cool is often just not worth it. The danger in letting your cool mind become a hot mind in this situation is that the other driver may have a gun on their front seat. You would be better off suppressing your anger and then feeling proud of yourself that you kept a cool head. Unfortunately, however, emotions have the power to overwhelm our better selves.

As you saw in the examples from chapter 1, radical speech and all the extremism and aggression that come with it is a major outcome of losing our cool. Rather than encountering another driver, in our media-saturated world, we are more likely to come up against someone attacking our political beliefs, our religion, or our support of or opposition to the gun lobby. There is radical-attacking speech everywhere in our polarized, divided society these days. That is just what it is like to live in a politicized atmosphere dominated by radical speakers

But even so, radical speech, as such, does not mean anything significant if a person does not pay any attention to it. There has to be a connection between the radicalism of the speech and the audience's engagement with it. The key component that fuels radical hearing in this kind of environment arises from what I call the *personal endorsement process.* If a person hears or reads something inflammatory and divisive, that simple exposure does not necessarily lead them to become influenced by it. There are ways to avoid falling victim to radical speech, and I describe these in chapter 9. A person can hear something, and even believe it and think that it is true, but that does not necessarily mean that they will actually meld it into their own personal way of thinking and believing. Personal endorsement is the key mechanism that leads people to adopt that speech as their own. Endorsement of this sort engages deep-lying psychological and emotional mechanisms. For someone to endorse something is to claim it as their own, to give it personal "ownership." This implies that this speech has become an important component of the *self.* The endorsement process is the key to the spread of radical hearing.

ENDORSING RADICAL SPEECH AND THE SELF-CONCEPT

Although the term *self* has many different shades of meaning, researchers characterize it as the constellation of our personal experiences, thoughts, beliefs, and commitments that constitute the "I," the "who I am" that we experience inwardly. It is the person behind the face that we see in the mirror, and it is the face we show to other people in our social world.

Endorsing a radical belief is an act that has significant personal consequences; believing it and claiming it as one's own gives it ownership. You own what you accept and what you believe; it becomes part of the "you." By agreeing with some radical stance, a person is in effect claiming it as a part of their belief system, and that in turn makes it a component of their *self.* But when radical beliefs are endorsed, they become infused with high levels of emotional meaning. Our self is our most valued, most emotional possession. This is why radical hearing is so dynamic and so emotionally loaded. To endorse a statement of opinion, radical or moderate, is to reflect the very nature of people's thoughts of who they *are.* But it is the endorsement of radical beliefs with their accompanying hostility and aggressiveness that has been such a significant source of our polarized social discourse. Since people's very definition of who they are becomes wedded to extreme beliefs, change becomes difficult and unlikely. This may be a key reason why, as Churchill says, fanatics can't change their mind and won't change the subject. To change beliefs would be to change the self, and that is very difficult. In the following chapters, I will show how radical beliefs slant and distort our judgment processes when dealing with "alien" beliefs and values and how, consequently, we reject moderation, ignore middle-ground distinctions, and rebuff anything that deviates from our emotional commitments.

Endorsing radical speech and adopting it as one's own begins with the process of *interiorization*, the bringing into the self of the norms, standards, beliefs, and behaviors of our social environment. In fact, sociologists consider interiorization to be a key to the socialization process whereby a newborn infant grows into a socialized adult. Psychologists have studied several types of cognitive factors involved in the endorsement process. Their findings give us particularly useful insight into how it is that endorsement, per se, leads radical hearers to adopt attitude positions that become so rigid and unyielding. Commitment to extreme beliefs leads people to resist changing those attitudes and beliefs. When is the last time you saw someone change one of their most deeply held beliefs? The fact that this occurs so rarely indicates the nature of what we are dealing with. I want to focus on the key elements of the way the endorsement process makes radical-hearing effects so deeply ingrained for the radical "true believer." I have surveyed various topics in the psychological research literature that illuminate some basic facets of the way the mind functions when it is exposed to radical speech. I have called this the "CVC" model of endorsement.

"C": The Dynamic Power of Freely Chosen Behavior

To start at the beginning of the interiorization process, it is obvious that people are not forced to become radical hearers. People are free to listen to whatever they please and to adopt any radical or moderate stance they choose, or they can ignore it all. In fact, under the US Constitution's Bill of Rights, it would be illegal to deny someone the right to speak, or to hear, statements of their own beliefs or those of someone else, no matter how radical. The First Amendment of the Constitution guarantees that "Congress shall make no law . . . abridging the freedom of speech, or of the press; or the right of the people peaceably to assemble . . ." That makes it pretty clear that radical speakers have little or no constraints on what they can say, no matter how polarizing or divisive it might be. On the other hand, the Constitution says nothing about the right of radical hearing, so we can presume that under the Bill of Rights people are free to listen to just about any speaker and to hear anything they choose to hear. Free speech is guaranteed and so, therefore, is radical hearing. It is legal, and it can be adopted by anyone, anytime, anyplace—and any issue is fair game. That might be why we have so many different issues where radical speech has helped to spread dissension and discord throughout our society.

Legalities aside, thinking of the interiorization process, this logic raises the issue of *free choice*, a topic of great interest to psychologists. It is the first step in the endorsement process, and we need to study it closely. Choosing our beliefs or choosing to endorse someone else's is an act of asserting, ultimately, our self.

From what psychologists know about the internal and external causes of behavior, attempting to force someone to believe something simply does not make sense. Dictators may be able to beat people into submitting to their way of doing things, but research is quite clear that forced compliance does not lead to inner acceptance. History is filled with instances in which force was used to make subject populations endorse the leader's beliefs. This may work in the short-term, but only for coercing overt behavior, and it will not work for establishing genuinely accepted true beliefs. And when the leader is removed and the force eliminated, then the original beliefs are restored. Forcing people to believe something that they do not want to believe is one of the main causes of revolutions. In recent Russian history, for example, the Communist Party did its best to ban all forms of religious observance, but the minute the party lost control of the government, the churches were nearly overwhelmed by the rush of people seeking to engage in their religious activities again. The pressure to "not believe" had no effect on true beliefs.

There are psychological, cognitive reasons why attitudes cannot be changed very well under high levels of external force. Psychologist Jack Brehm has developed a cognitive model of this effect.[1] His concept of "psychological reactance" proposes that when a person's choice of holding a particular belief is threatened by some external force, then a motivated state of resistance—reactance—arises against that threat. According to Brehm, people will go to great lengths to react against a threat to their behavioral freedom, for example, the freedom to accept what a radical speaker is saying. As a consequence of that resistance, the belief is maintained and can even become stronger.

Stephen Worchel and Jack Brehm conducted experiments on reactance.[2] In this study, the subjects were given a set of statements concerning public policy: whether the government should discriminate against the Communist Party. But the statements were accompanied with instructions stating, "You have no choice but to believe this" or "You cannot believe otherwise." In the experiment, not only did people not accept such policy statements as their own; they reacted against them and rated negatively to the idea of restriction. This was true even for those people who *were* against the idea of restricting the Communist Party. But, even more interesting, people who thought that communists should not be discriminated against believed it *less* after they thought that they were about to be forced to believe it. People have a tendency to react against pressure that threatens their freedom of actions.

Does this sound familiar? During the Revolutionary War, Americans adopted a widely used slogan, "Don't Tread on Me," a beautiful statement of reactance. Perhaps even more vivid is the motto of the state of New Hampshire, "Live Free or Die." The American people seem to have reactance built into their social genes, as the British found out in the Revolutionary War, and as Japan discovered after their attack on Pearl Harbor. Both nations got wars in return for their threats to Americans' freedom.

Reactance extends even to politeness in our social relationships. In another study, Jack Brehm and Ann Cole showed that people tend to not return a favor to someone (in this case, a research aide) who had unexpectedly done them a favor.[3] By previous arrangement, the research aide gave the experiment participants a soda without saying anything; he just did them a favor without being asked to do so. A bit later in the experiment, the participants were given an opportunity to offer a soda to the research aide, but they ignored that opportunity, making no attempt to return the favor. The fact that the soda had not been requested or freely chosen by the participants appeared to put some pressure on them to reciprocate, and so they resisted.

So a model that proposes that people become radical hearers because they are somehow forced to do so has little historical or research evidence to support it, and, in fact, there is considerable evidence against it. The more likely interpretation is that people become radical hearers because they want to, because they choose to, because there is something compatible between the radical speech they are hearing and their own personal attributes and characteristics.

"V": The Role of Valuing

Research has shown that there is a close connection between the choices we make and our values. In short, studies show that we do what we like, and if we have done something freely, then we will come to like it. Generally speaking, this link between doing and valuing is a bidirectional relationship. We tend to choose things that we value, and our choices to do something can cause us to value them more highly, as my colleague Alex Zautra and I have shown.[4] This is where we can see radical hearing at its root beginnings. The logic goes like this: if we choose to endorse radical speech, then we value that choice *because* we made it, and our beliefs and values incorporate it into our self-concept.

Let me give some research-based examples of this choice/valuing link. My first example is a particularly prevalent one: gambling. Although the topic might not at first seem relevant to my points about radical hearing, the underlying principles are the same. Gambling is thought of as a game, so it should be highly valued, and it is by some people. But it is a game in which the odds are very much stacked against the player. Losing money, as bad as that outcome is, is a high-likelihood outcome for most of us. If there is anything that you cannot control, it is luck and chance. No one is forced to gamble, so it is clearly a matter of personal choice. Since games of chance themselves are by definition not something we control, and since winning is not something that one can make happen (unless they cheat), why would people even try to control such games? But they do, often in very colorful ways. Players blow on their dice, throw them at a certain angle, talk to them, pray over them. This is what sociologist James Henslin calls "craps and magic" in his study of Chicago-area cab drivers who spent their spare time playing craps.[5] People are engaging in magical thinking here, but that does not make it any less compelling to them. In this way, playing slot machines is psychologically identical to dice throwing. Players will pull down the handle with a certain force and speed, or they will wear their lucky hat, as if these things could change the electronic wiring behind the flashing lights and jingling bells. Their choice to play the game no doubt gives them a positive feeling and raises their confidence in winning. In fact, losing really does not have much of an effect; they believe that Lady Luck will certainly come their way if they just keep at it. In a study I will discuss shortly, the more people who suffer a poor outcome after having made a freely chosen act, the higher the psychological pressure is to value it even more. No wonder people who choose extremist beliefs hold on to them so tightly, even as they see their society dividing and polarizing right in front of them.

Psychology researcher Ellen Langer has devoted many years to studying the psychology of gambling, examining exactly this aspect of the activity. She tested directly the choice/valuing connection in her study of lottery ticket players.[6] Her experimental setup was quite simple. She went to two companies whose employees traditionally held various drawings and had cash pools for betting on sports contests. These employees were used to gambling, so Langer had no trouble recruiting them to be in her study. The employees were randomly assigned to two conditions. In the "high-choice" condition, the employees were asked if they wished to participate in the lottery and pay $1 for a ticket (that price is important to remember). If they agreed to participate, they were presented with a box of lottery tickets and asked to pick one. That card number was noted, and an identical ticket was dropped into the lottery box. In the other "low-choice" condition, employees were simply handed a lottery ticket. In actuality, all experimental conditions were identical, since those in the group who were handed their tickets were also asked to pay $1

On the morning of the lottery drawing, each participant was approached by Langer, who told them, "Someone in the other office wanted to get into the lottery, but since I'm not selling tickets anymore, he asked me if I'd find out how much you'd sell your ticket for. It makes no difference to me, but how much should I tell him?"[7]

The results of the study were striking. The two groups felt very differently about selling back their tickets to Langer. The high-choice group participants wanted to charge an average of $8.67 for their tickets, whereas the no-choice participants charged an average of $1.96 for theirs! Langer then asked them directly if they would sell their tickets. As you might guess from the above results, 37 percent of the high-choice participants refused to sell their tickets, while only 19 percent of the low-choice group refused; they valued their tickets much less and were more willing to part with them. Remember that they all paid $1 for a ticket. The only thing that varied between the two groups was the degree of choice they asserted over obtaining their tickets.

A different angle on the choice issue is seen in a real-world case of winning a windfall prize of money. Researcher Hal Arkes and his colleagues, studying unexpected gains, relayed a human-interest story about a publishing firm that distributed sales commissions and a surprise bonus at its annual meeting in the Bahamas.[8] All sales employees were given a bonus of $50, a significant amount at the time. Near their hotel was a casino. Most of the people who had received a bonus gambled their money at the casino (there was no report on their success). An interesting quote comes from a disappointed employee, Nancy, who was upset about losing all her money in the casino: "If I hadn't been given the $50, there's no way I would have spent a dime at the casino. There are plenty of things I could have used the money for. Why did I waste it?"[9] She wasted it because she did not value it enough, and to be given something with no choice or personal effort seems to lead to devaluation. You do not waste what you value. Daniel Kahneman has labeled this valuing process "the endowment effect."[10]

"C": The Role of the Commitment Process

In addition to enhancing value, freely choosing a course of action has another mental consequence that makes it a particularly useful concept for understanding radical hearing. Choice tends to increase our valuing of the act or belief that we have chosen, and research shows that *commitment* to the beliefs or actions that we have freely made will make the behavior "stick." If we are committed to something we freely choose, then our cognitive and behavioral tendencies will line up to make us stick to that choice strongly. This "stickiness" is a hallmark of extremism. Even more, radicals will stick with their committed beliefs and actions even in the face of evidence that goes counter to their beliefs and values. Gamblers will keep right on engaging in the same activity in spite of evidence that they are losing money. Maybe I am too cheap, but the mere thought of losing money with nothing to show for it is really upsetting to me. I once asked a confirmed gambler what went through his mind when he saw his money disappearing. His casual reply: "Oh, it just doesn't matter, I'll make it back." So his valuing/commitment button, if there is such a thing, simply ignored the obvious fact that his money was gone. You and I would say on rational considerations of statistical probability that the money is not coming back, but he continued to engage in the highly valued, freely chosen gambling behavior, losses be damned. Message: beware of your commitments, especially when money is involved.

The effect of what happens in the face of directly disconfirming evidence and consequent unpleasant outcomes of our choices was reported by Leon Festinger, Henry Riecken, and Stanley Schachter in their classic study of a religious cult predicting the end of the world.[11] Since the world is still here, you can see the outcome of their predictions, but it is the psychological consequence of that "disconfirmation" that has been so important in our understanding of free choice.

The story came about when a religious cult in Chicago gained notoriety from their prediction that the end of the world was coming that November. The researchers joined in the group's activities to observe the dynamics of how the members were going to prepare for "the end." The leader of the group, Ms. Keech (an alias), was quite charismatic and totally dedicated to preparing her flock for the coming of the Lord, who had promised to send a gigantic flood to the earth to cleanse it of its sins. However, he had been so impressed with "The Seekers" (as the group was known), that on the appointed day of doom he promised to send down a rocket ship to save them. This message was printed in the local newspapers, and the publicity led to new members joining the group (willingly, of course) in order to be saved. Many of the members were quite fervent in their beliefs, so much so that some of them quit their jobs and gave away most of their worldly possessions in preparation of the coming flood. (Who needs possessions in heaven?)

On the appointed day of the flood, the congregation gathered at the home of Ms. Keech and began praying in anticipation of the arrival of the rocket. Their anxiety and joy about the upcoming salvation reached a pitch late in the evening, with the rocket due to arrive at any moment. But ten o'clock came, eleven o'clock came, then midnight, and still no rocket was in sight! Tension began to give way to dismay. At 2 a.m., Ms. Keech retired to her room to pray to hear from the Lord. (In the meantime, Mr. Keech, who was not a believer, went to bed and slept through the night's events.) At four o'clock in the morning, Ms. Keech returned to the distressed members and with great joy and enthusiasm said that she had just had a revelation from God. He decreed that he had been so impressed with the dedication and faith of the church flock that he had called off the flood! Their faith had saved themselves and the world.

In *When Prophecy Fails*, Festinger, Riecken, and Schachter wrote up their observations about this event and what happened as a result of the "failure of prediction." From a psychological perspective, the book is a fascinating study in commitment. You might think that people who had had their beliefs so directly contradicted by reality would change their minds about their beliefs and maybe even quit the church and go on with the rest of their lives. But the authors found just that the opposite was true! Although some members did leave, apparently chagrined and embarrassed, the majority of the church members became even more fervent, even more sure that God was looking out for them, and even more sure that God would indeed still send the flood, just sometime in the future. If you keep up with the national news, this sort of story gets played out every year or so. As I will say later in this chapter, the human mind has a need for structure and certainty, and these sorts of millennial beliefs can fulfill that role for some people.

How can direct disconfirmation of what we have chosen to believe not make us change our beliefs? Changing our attitudes is difficult, but if direct, slap-in-the-face facts do not change us, what will? As the authors proposed, and as I showed earlier, it is the act of freely choosing to believe something that gives it personal meaning and encourages a strong personal commitment to it. If we behave according to our beliefs, and if we are motivated to keep our beliefs and our public face consistent with each other, then we become strongly committed to that belief. In fact, disconfirmation serves only to strengthen the connection between our belief in our self and our choices. It would create a state of cognitive dissonance if we were to think that our belief was wrong or foolish, so to keep cognitive consonance, we continue to think that we were right in the first place. How often do you see some radical person saying that they were wrong? It is a rare thing indeed. So, in short, free choice creates value for the chosen belief, and that in turn creates personal, enduring commitment to that chosen alternative.

A more poignant but equally compelling view of the choice/value/commitment connection is seen in the amazing and tragic story of the Jonestown mass suicides in Guyana in 1978. The story is comprehensively reviewed by Neal Osherow.[12] Again, a charismatic religious leader, in this case the Reverend Jim Jones, was the center of an ever-expanding group of people who wanted to join his "church," the Peoples' Temple, in Oakland, California, in 1955. As the size and social importance of Jones's temple grew, so did his troubles with local authorities. Finally, he moved the entire temple of over nine hundred members to the state of Guyana on the northern coast of South America. Legal troubles continued to pursue him, culminating in an official visit by Congressman Leo Ryan from Jones's

Oakland district. Jones had his lieutenants murder Congressman Ryan and four of his companions as they attempted to board a plane after inspecting the site. Apparently fearing the consequences of that disaster, Jones then ordered his congregation—men, women, and children—to drink a cyanide-laced beverage. Nine hundred and eighteen people died, including Jones and most of his lieutenants; only a few people escaped to tell the world their story.

Although a host of mental and social forces combined to bring about this almost unbelievable event, I want to bring special attention to the initiating causal event here, the commitment the people made to join the church. I could not find any evidence that anyone was actually forced to join the temple. But once that initial commitment was freely made, then all the consequent events had a solid foundation on which their small, seemingly harmless effects could build. It was a step-by-step process of gradually greater and greater commitments that made the members become so fatally devoted to following Jones's desires. First, in spite of their poor economic status, members would tithe to the temple. Then they began performing small duties to help out around the temple. Then they made even greater commitments, such as donating their cars and household possessions. By the time Jones moved the temple to Guyana, its members had made so many small, step-by-step commitments that Jones's seriously disruptive decision to send them off to a foreign land was just one more step. But once in Guyana, they were thrown into a strange and unfamiliar environment, a jungle with little resemblance to their former lives. The only support they could get for their actions was a heavy reliance on each other and, of course, on the speech and leadership of Reverend Jones. There is no doubt that in addition to the trail of commitments they had made, the social pressures of the fellow congregants to go along must have had a powerful influence on their adjustment to the situation, a point made clearly by my colleague Robert Cialdini in his groundbreaking book, *Influence*.[13] But most people need to keep a tight, emotional hold on their beliefs, even in the face of certain death. The effects of radical hearing are rarely so extreme, but the motivational states resulting from freely choosing what to believe are what get the beliefs embedded deeply in people's minds and essentially set in stone. Swallowing poison can be seen as only one more step in a long sequence of justifying our beliefs with our choices, sustaining the power of the original commitment. I will raise this issue again chapter 10, where I describe why it is unrealistic to expect radical hearers to change their beliefs. We may have to live with divisiveness and polarization, but changing those things will not be easy.

EMBEDDEDNESS AND THE SELF-CONCEPT

At the end of the chain of free choice and valuing comes a process of embedding of the commitment, or integrating the belief into the person's overall psychological makeup. Social psychologists Douglas Kenrick, Steven Neuberg, and Robert Cialdini have described the process this way: "A strongly held attitude is more embedded in (connected to) additional features of the person, such as the individual's self-concept, values, and social identity."[14]

To study the embeddedness process itself, Eva Pomerantz, Shelly Chaiken, and Rosalind Tordesillas studied people's attitudes about several hot-button social issues such as capital punishment, legalized abortion, and environmental protection, investigating the relatedness of those attitudes to how biased the people were in thinking about the topics, how central or important their beliefs were to their self-concepts, and how resistant those beliefs were to being changed by new information.[15] They found a high degree of interrelatedness of these personal belief components. The tight relationships were captured by two major statistical dimensions of attitude strength: embeddedness and commitment. These factors were in fact correlated with each other, and it was found that they both contributed to the attitudes becoming resistant to being changed. When strongly held beliefs become embedded into our ideas of who we are, then a whole network of other mental processes becomes linked and intertwined, making us committed to them and very resistant to changing them.

In fact, recent evidence is starting to show that attitudes and political behavior may well have genetic and physiological traits that make them highly stable and resistant to change because of their biological foundations. Partisan beliefs have been shown by Christopher Dawes and James Fowler to be related to certain chemical receptors in the brain,[16] and Dawes and Fowler, along with Laura Baker, report that genetic twins have more similar attitudes of partisanship than nontwins.[17] Later, I will use such evidence to explain why changing radical-hearing effects is going to be such a difficult challenge for our polarized society.

NEEDING STRUCTURE IN OUR THINKING AND JUDGING

Returning to the story of Jim Jones for a moment, moving to the jungle of Guyana from the very urban world of Oakland, California, must have been very unsettling for the temple members, all of them city dwellers. Following the powerful words of Jones must have been comforting for them, and when he called for everyone to drink the poison, the step must not have seemed very different from all the previous freely chosen behaviors. There is a significant cognitive issue here, and I want to elaborate on what it says about the mental context and broader properties of radical hearing.

Our self-concept is particularly sensitive to what researchers call "epistemic motivation" (from the Greek word *episteme*, generally translated to mean "to know"). There is a fundamental human need for structure, organization, and predictability in the way we understand things. This is a motivated need, a drive to need to know, to understand, to be clear about what's going on. On the other side, to have our information about our world restricted, reduced, or eliminated is indeed destructive and upsetting. The classic research shows that sensory deprivation (putting a blindfold on someone, putting them into a completely dark room, and so on) is highly stressful and certainly is something to be avoided. Coming home to your dark house at night after a movie can be scary until you turn on the light. You need to see where you are going; you need to know your environment, to have it "structured." Interestingly, researchers think of this as an organismic need. That is, all living creatures show motivated drives to explore their environment, to develop habits and structured responses that help reduce randomness and disorder in their adaptation to their world. Evolutionarily, this has proven to be a successful tactic for organisms to survive and prosper. That may be why it is so universal.

PERSONALITY TRAITS AND THE NEED FOR STRUCTURE

Although the need to know is universal in organisms, it is not *fixed*: we are not all identical in how we evolved our individual ways of perceiving and responding to the world. Researchers have explored this issue with their concept of *cognitive simplicity/complexity*. This is the degree to which a person is capable of making subtle distinctions, careful articulations between different stimuli, as opposed to simple, quick, undifferentiated, and rigid responses. It is the ability to keep multiple alternatives in mind simultaneously. You do not find these properties in radical hearing. One of the early researchers on this topic, William Scott, defined cognitive complexity as a measure of the extent to which a person maintains separateness among his or her cognitions about a given topic.[18] If a person's thoughts about a given topic are redundant with each other or are grouped together rather than functioning separately and distinctively, then that is what he calls "dimensionality." That is a useful view of cognitive simplicity. It implies that in the florid language a radical speaker throws at an enemy, there may be underlying cognitive simplicity in the same simple point being made over and over. One has to get beyond the verbal barrage and look for the underlying cognitive simplicity (in Scott's case, a lack of high dimensionality). This is a revealing approach to radical hearing. In this language, a complex thinker can perceive differences and yet find ways to integrate those distinctions into a larger, more complex set, as opposed to merely having redundant, uninformative distinctions. Business and psychology educator Patricia Linville followed up this idea with studies on cognitive simplicity/complexity and found that less complexity is correlated with more extreme, more polarized attitudes.[19]

Researchers Marc Hetherington and Jonathan Weiler have shown that this type of personality characteristic provides a good description of a significant difference between the major political parties in American society today.[20] Philip Tetlock has investigated the actual public statements of political figures, including members of the British Parliament, politicians during the World War I era, and American senators.[21] His method analyzes two distinct components of what people actually say: the number of separate dimensions or factors in the distinctions that they see, and the degree to which those distinctions are connected with each other. Both components considered together create a score of what he calls *integrative complexity*. Extreme conservatives and extreme liberals score lower on integrative complexity than do more moderate conservatives and liberals.[22] Senators who supported isolationism and withdrawal from international relations scored lower in integrative complexity.

It is important to note one major feature of this approach to thinking processes. It emphasizes the *structure* of people's thoughts and beliefs, *not the content* of those thoughts and beliefs. A person can be cognitively complex or cognitively simple regarding any particular set of cognitions, be it political, religious, social policy, and so on. In this sense, it is a general approach to cognitive processes. O. J. Harvey, David Hunt, and Harold Schroder in fact proposed that a person's personality should best be thought of as a *system* of cognitions, varying from simple and concrete to complex and abstract.[23] Approaching the idea as a system, we need to investigate the interactions linking our cognitions and our judgments of our social relationships as well. When these all move to a condition of simplicity, rather than of complexity, then we have a stabilized network of the effects of radical hearing to embed. Regarding personality as a system has been a powerful way to look at the ways radical hearing can have divisive effects.

As I will show, however, you can get very similar simplifying and rigidifying effects when emotions enter a person's cognitive system. Cognitive simplicity is one of the key hallmarks of hot emotions and deeply held beliefs. One prime example of this is religion, where our beliefs and commitments become fused with intense emotions. For instance, as shown by researchers B. Jack White and O. J. Harvey, people who tend toward more cognitively simple beliefs see fewer distinctions, and they make more extremist judgments when they are emotionally involved with their religious beliefs.[24] Religion is one good dividing line; it provides the external structure and order some people seek, while other people reject it for that reason. And of course religion is one of the major hot-button issues in human history.

Understanding this type of mental characteristic goes a long way toward explaining why people have trouble tolerating each other. The term "a simple-minded person" may sound denigrating, but in fact, in the language of the science of judgment processes, it is actually quite descriptive. When people employ simple two-category thinking, then that is in fact direct evidence of simple-minded cognitive processes. Later chapters will discuss research on judgmental processes that show exactly that: two-category thinking driven by assimilation and contrast effects. Self-concept processes develop and harden around central ways of thinking and believing, and these processes provide structure and anchorage points when we make judgments about other people and their beliefs. Indeed, the certainty that one is right and that "the other" is wrong provides all the armor one needs to reject the beliefs of someone who is different. Unfortunately for society, this also happens when the other person is more moderate and is not as committed to battle as the radical hearer is. I will show evidence of this in later chapters.

Moderation is in "the middle," and therein lies its ambiguity, its lack of definiteness. The middle ground is "gray" in a true believer's mental world, who sees only black versus white, good versus bad, mine versus the other. Of course, the middle ground is where the extremists *could* come to negotiate their differences and work toward finding a mutually satisfying solution to the problems that divide them from each other and from moderates. But if an emotionally involved person cannot even understand or accept a moderate's position in the first place—and evidence presented in this book shows that they cannot—then there are no grounds for accommodation and successful problem solving. Cognitively, then, this is one major reason why voices of moderation can't be heard.

MOTIVATED REASONING PROCESSES

Researchers have pinpointed a key component of this process. Our reasoning processes are slanted by a particular type of cognitive orientation. It engages when we are confronted by new or different information, particularly when this information is related to our own system of beliefs. There are two emotion-based processes that start functioning when we are exposed to new information. One process is a motivated striving to be accurate in what we think about a topic. We need to be well-informed and to know what is going on. Given that sort of rational process, we should expect a person to want to learn the new information so they can be better informed and be better able to respond accurately and appropriately to the new issue.

But research shows that that nice idea is too simple. When confronted with new information or the pressure to go outside of our boundaries, the second process takes over; this process involves our attitudes and emotions. The accuracy of our perceptions depends on the "fit" between new information and preexisting attitudes and emotional commitment about the topic. If there is not a close fit or congruence between our current thinking and the new information, then a separate motivation to handle the lack of fit becomes engaged. A study by Charles Lord, Lee Ross, and Mark Lepper investigated the reactions that people have to communications (messages) about studies either supporting or refuting the value of the death penalty in deterring crimes of murder.[25] They assessed participants' attitudes about this hot-button issue at the start of their study. Then they gave the participants a set of printed arguments about this issue. The arguments were presented as summaries of statistical studies and were then followed by detailed descriptions of the studies, which gave them a convincing aura of scientific authenticity. At the end of the testing, the participants were asked to again rate their personal opinions about the issue as well as how convincing they found the new evidence to be. The key to the study was that all participants read and rated all supporting and refuting messages, so that in effect they had to process information that both supported and attacked their initial opinion. The results of the study showed clear evidence of biased information processing by the participants. Those who were initially in favor of the death penalty became even more in favor, and those who initially opposed it became even more opposed to it. No big news there; the mind seeks out and responds to congruence or balance between current condition and new information.

But the investigators were also interested in how the participants perceived the grounds of the arguments they had been given. The participants were asked to rate the convincingness of the messages they had been given. As you might expect, the messages supporting their initial opinions were rated as more "convincing" than the messages on the opposite side of the issue. You might think that a person who reads a message opposing their own personal opinion, with supportive scientific evidence, would become more uncertain in their own beliefs and would become less attitudinally extreme, but that is not how biased judgment processes actually operate. The results of the study showed just the opposite. In fact, the authors concluded that the net result of having people who hold opposite attitudes become exposed to counter-attitudinal information is that it makes them become even more oppositional and polarized than they were before the study began. This is a neat demonstration of Jack Brehm's psychological reactance effect, as it shows not only a counterreaction to messages intended to change our attitudes, but it also shows that the mind undercuts and rejects the grounds on which our opponents stand—even scientific grounds.

That study also shows a bias in cool, rational information processing; as presented in these studies, it is a purely cognitive, information-biased processing. But people are also motivated to keep their beliefs intact and consistent with their emotional commitments. Psychologists call this source of bias "motivated reasoning." This label is applied to a large body of studies that show several linked aspects of the thoughts and perceptions that people engage when dealing with issues and topics that are important to them. Much of this fascinating work is summarized by Ziva Kunda.[26]

Studies have repeatedly shown that emotional commitments trump the "cooler," more rational part of our judgments. Robert Zajonc coined the classic phrase "affect is primary" to summarize a large body of research that shows that what we *feel* precedes what we *think*.[27] Basically, we are at the end of someone's mental processing by the time *we* find out what they believe; that person's emotion system has already become engaged and is already biasing their thoughts and responses. A similar model has appeared in the cognitive heuristics literature pioneered by Kahneman and Tversky, cited earlier in this chapter. Paul Slovic, Melissa Finucane, Ellen Peters, and Donald MacGregor have proposed the concept of "affect heuristic."[28] This short-cut mental device biases our decisions about risks and hazards when our feelings about some choice cause us to miss important information. For instance, if we feel good about some aspect of the choice, that feeling itself can lead us to underrate the riskiness of the decision or to overrate its benefits. This can lead us to work against our own self-interest. Although I do not deal with perceptions of risks or hazards in this book, the concept that affect is primary is certainly a compatible way of thinking about judgment processes.

So the effect of trying to get people to think about and judge topics that are touchy and emotionally significant parts of their belief systems will lead them to process only new information that *is in line with* what they already feel and believe. That is called *confirmation bias*; we want to be reassured that what we believe is supported by the evidence. We want our self-concept and our mental structuring processes to be affirmed and supported by our experiences and by any new information we receive. On the other side of this coin, we tend to ignore or actively reject information that does not fit our preexisting beliefs and emotional commitments. This is called *disconfirmation bias*, in that we have a bias against evidence that might disconfirm what we want to believe. If possible, we will choose to ignore it, or, if we cannot avoid it, we will actively criticize it and reject it as wrong.

For instance, a smoker can and will find a dozen reasons why he or she will not get cancer from smoking. People do not want to believe that they are vulnerable to threat, so they easily come up with many reasons to support their sense of invulnerability. Alcoholics will deny that they have a drinking problem—and will deny it and deny it until something finally breaks into that structured, rigid set of beliefs. There may be many various excuses and beliefs, but there is only one category: "I don't have a problem, so don't bother me." Nothing is so comforting as a made-up mind, even when the person is going down because of it.

Charles Taber and Milton Lodge call this "motivated skepticism."[29] As they say, we are not able to control our preconceptions, and those preconceptions set us up for inevitable biases in judging our own beliefs and those of others. In their study on this issue, they presented their research participants with short "pro" and "con" paragraphs on two emotionally hot issues, affirmative action and gun control. The participants were asked to choose which paragraphs they wanted to read. For both issues, participants overwhelmingly chose to read paragraphs supporting their own side of the issue and to avoid reading paragraphs that represented the opposition side of their issues. So we simply do not want to expose ourselves to opposing points of view. We decline to even look at our opponent's point of view, let alone process it very deeply.

The study by Pomerantz, Chaiken, and Tordesillas, discussed earlier in this chapter, neatly shows how this sort of bias arises when the issue is emotionally arousing.[30] The researchers showed that people who have a strong attitude about capital punishment rejected the arguments opposite to their beliefs that were presented to them by the experimenters. In rejecting opponents' beliefs, they claimed that those opposing arguments were biased and methodologically flawed. The participants rated down the convincingness of the evidence attacking their stand on the issue of the death penalty. These results must sound familiar to anyone reading the news these days. These same types of processes are occurring in our current national debate about global warming and climate change. People who do not want government trying to change our environmental behaviors tend to disbelieve the basic science valued by those who do believe that policies have to be changed; they are just not convinced by whatever evidence is used to support the position they dislike. Any science used by members of the other side to bolster their arguments is immediately not convincing to the opponents, because their strong beliefs lead them to disbelieve the very science that would otherwise be convincing to someone less cognitively and less emotionally committed.

Most research on attitudes and beliefs has found a relationship between how strongly an attitude is held and how intensely it is believed, as well as the resistance of that attitude to any attempts to change it. Even flatly contradictory evidence has little or no effect on people's beliefs. For example, some people believe that autism is a direct result of childhood immunizations, and they deny evidence to the contrary. Others are not convinced by virtually any evidence that men landed on the moon in America's space exploration program. Still others believe that herbs can cure cancer, but the evidence on that will be questioned by people who think that cures lie in better science and medicine.

Neither you nor I need to get involved in these thorny social issues at this point. What I want to do with these examples is to make a simple point and a complex point. The simple point is that people are often extraordinarily difficult to convince of positions contrary to their own: opposing evidence can get no traction because these people do not accept the grounds on which the opposing positions are based (chapter 6 presents a detailed discussion of more research of this problem). But there is a more complex issue here. A major psychological reason why fanatics can't change their minds (as stated by Winston Churchill) is because strong attitudes give us certainty; they give us structure and meaning in our world, providing clear guidance while warding off uncertainty and ambiguity. One notable feature of strongly involved radical hearers is that they are always certain, clear, and consistent. Such qualities can be a powerful inducement to people experiencing stressful circumstances. An example of such a situation is what happened to German citizens after World War I. Adolf Hitler preached the certainty of a better future to his dispirited and—I would add—uncertain citizens. His words must have had a magnetizing influence to ward off the horrors of what happened to his country in the aftermath of the Great War. The need for structure and certainty is surely one of the keys to motivated reasoning and disconfirmation biases underlying our thoughts, our emotions, and our actions.

Obviously, all these biases will work against social unity. Hoping that people will naturally get along with each other just does not describe how we actually live. Social unity has to face the opposition of our deeply embedded mental-processing tendencies. To some significant degree, our minds work against us in being open and fair-minded when we consider beliefs different from our own; this is certainly the case when our emotions are aroused by hot-button, emotional topics. Voices of moderation cannot be heard in these circumstances, when emotion warps what we hear. The emotionally biased mind of the partisan seeks cognitive simplicity, clarity, certitude, and orderliness; it has no time or energy for processing subtle, fine-grained distinctions. But that is where moderation lies and where we can find common ground if we will exert the cognitive effort to open up our thinking processes to the value of seriously listening to different voices.

CHAPTER 3

JUDGING AND (MIS)PERCEIVING THE WORLD

When we take an impartial, objective look at our current society, we have to wonder, how *could* it happen? How could there be such divisiveness and polarization over issue after issue? How could ordinarily moderate people come to show such hatred, such aggression, such derogatory and punitive attitudes and opinions about their fellow citizens? It might make sense if they were involved in war, if they felt their very survival were threatened by the actions of "the enemy." But physical survival is rarely at stake when we consider the kinds of issues and sentiments expressed by the quotations presented in chapter 1. Certainly the issues are important, even critical, in some sense, but for people to feel such extreme prejudice and hostility toward those who believe differently from them causes one to ask "What's going on here?"

What is going on here are the consequences of human emotions—emotions that erupt when political, religious, or social issues get embedded in the radical person's very self-concept, when people become *ego-involved*. Once a person's self-concept gets threatened, then all our emotional feelings and behaviors boil up. Emotions narrow our perspective, they arm us for a fight-or-flight response, and they can disrupt careful, deliberative thinking. But it is more than that. We have to go to the source of the discontent.

We will not gain much traction for eliminating our social divisions if we concentrate too much on radical speakers and the prominent opinion formers who receive so much media coverage. They are the ones who reinforce and spread the divisiveness of radical speech throughout the society. They continue the cycle of attack-response-counterattack, which is the main social dynamic that is driving us apart. But I take the position that radical speakers are not the most important source of our discontent. We need to go one step further, to the audience who is exposed to such speech. There we can look inside the thinking processes of those who listen to the speech and those who become partisan, committed believers in what the radical speakers are saying. The individual person who actively pays attention to the speech of radicals and who comes to believe and adopt those extremist ideas is the key to our understanding of what is happening to our social unity. Individuals—perhaps you and me—are the ones who endorse and come to believe radical speech and who become radical hearers, with all that that entails. But individuals are the ones who can change things if we can find the will to do something about it.

If we want to understand this process better, and especially if we want to do something about our divisiveness, we have to look at the core of radical hearing's effects. That core is based in the fundamental workings of the human mind, particularly in human judgment and decision-making processes. And that is why I have focused this book on the process of judgment. In this chapter, I present a general orientation to this key concept and how it works in our daily living. This is a special view of thinking processes, and this view has given us a wealth of insights into how we become divided from each other. Unfortunately, while psychological researchers understand very well how these processes work and have written extensively about them in their technical journals and books, the lay public and our leaders have no knowledge of any of this research. But the public is where the action is when it comes to these processes, so this book will describe for all members of our society—and any society—the fundamental principles and the implications of research studies that show quite clearly how our minds are biased by radical hearing.

First, I will define and characterize some basic principles of judgment that are at the foundations of how radical hearing operates for the individual person. This will allow me to review one of the most remarkable developments in the social sciences: the science of *psycho-*

physics. It is an amazing discovery, and from it we can understand how it is that hot-button emotions affect how we think about and respond to each other. Considering this foundational body of research, I can then show how it has been extended into many different areas of our daily living, among which are the poisonous judgments we make about other people's beliefs.

JUDGMENT IS THE KEY TO REVEALING MENTAL LIFE

How are we to understand the psychology of bias and radical hearing? People's mental lives are not immediately available; we stand as outsiders to them, able only to observe the overt ways they conduct their lives. We can't "know" them like we "know" ourselves because we do not have what philosophers call privileged access, which we do have for our own mental lives. But we can get reports of what other people are thinking and feeling, and we can observe their judgment and decision processes, and from them infer their underlying mental status. Consequently, psychologists have converged on the importance of understanding the process of judgment as offering the key insight into understanding a person's mental life. In my approach, judgment is the key to understanding radical hearing. The following definition from Merriam-Webster highlights the facets of the term that are most useful for my purposes here:

> Judgment (noun): the process of forming an opinion or evaluation by discerning and comparing.

I use this particular definition because it refers to the processes of "discerning" and "comparing." The discernment process can be thought of as the ability of the mind to grasp something, one thing, as an entity, as a separate event or thing that can be distinguished as different from another. The breakdown of discernment is shown when a person cannot tell the difference between one thing and another. This sounds pretty scary, especially when we see such a breakdown expressed in everyday statements like "all Republicans are right-wingers" or "all Democrats are tax-and-spend liberals." Politicians build careers on lumping their opponents into one single "discernment," one with, of course, a negative label attached to it. In the context of our public discourse, it is in the "hearing, thinking, and judging" process that people come to agree or to disagree with what radical speakers are saying.

Research on discerning and comparing is based on one fundamental principle: *There is no such thing as absolute judgment; all judgment is relative.* Judgment is extraordinarily sensitive to influences coming from a person's individual store of cognitive, emotional, and social resources. In effect, the judgment process works very much like a Geiger counter: it detects even small amounts of "radiation"; in this example, the toxic radiation of radical speech. In addition, judgment is *comparative*. Any thoughts and decisions we make are based on comparing and contrasting each (new) experience we have against a context or background of our other thoughts and experiences, our opinions and attitudes. Much like a movie set's background scene against which actors perform, our own personal backgrounds color and bias any new information that we experience. It is as if the "radiation" has soaked into the very stage scenery of our perceptual and judgmental process, coloring it and giving it meaning to us. The foreground action, the movements and lines of the actors, can result in biased perceptions of the meaning of the action onstage. For example, imagine that you hear someone (an actor reciting his lines) say "I want my people to have a better society." That is a wonderful statement, proposing an admirable and worthwhile goal. But what if, as you look at the scenery behind the actor, you see a Nazi swastika? The meaning of that actor's statement is automatically colored by the listener. If the listener is a Nazi supporter, it is a wonderful sentiment. But if the listener is a British citizen whose city is being bombed by German forces, then that person will experience a very different set of thoughts about the same statement. The background determines the inferred meaning of the statement, just as our own background of emotions prejudices what we hear from our friends and our opponents, supporting and contaminating future processing.

THE CONCEPT OF REFERENCE SCALE

Psychological science has developed a term for this critical process: the *reference scale*. Psychologists define this concept as the mental framework against which any input stimulus is compared; the "meaning" of any event is derived from its comparison with the set of judgment categories that constitutes our personal reference scale. Our reference scales organize and systematize our perceptions, giving us immediate understanding of the meaning and value of an experience.

A reference scale is a set of separate distinctions that help us organize and understand our experiences. These distinctions can be thought of as cognitive categories that group and organize our perceptions of the similarities and differences we perceive as we make judgments about the meanings of the various elements of our perceptual world. If a person detects a difference between one stimulus and another, then there is discrimination, and there is therefore a judgment category for detecting that difference. For example, deeply religious people differ from nonbelievers in their judgments about beliefs in a "higher power." They would surely differ in their judgments of how positive or negative the statement "God is an interesting concept" is to a belief in God. Believers would regard such a statement as virtual heresy because it is suspiciously weak (treating God as a concept rather than as a reality), whereas nonbelievers might judge it as sounding too favorable, perhaps dangerously so. Both types of people have a reference scale of "degree of belief," but these scales operate very differently. If we are to get a handle on radical speech and radical hearing, we have to understand the basic principles that underlie the judgment processes of these people when emotional commitments are high.

THE PHYSICAL PERSONAL REFERENCE SCALE

The importance of how personal experiences and perspectives become involved in perceiving a stimulus was demonstrated in an early and very clever study on reference scales by Margaret Tresselt.[1] She asked people with two very different kinds of lifestyle backgrounds to be participants in a simple weight-lifting judgment study. One group comprised thirty-five professional jewelers from New York City, and the other was made up of thirty-five men, some professional weightlifters and some who were at an advanced level of weight training. If our principles of psychological judgment are valid, the background experiences of each group should transfer to their performance in the laboratory and demonstrate a systematic biasing of their judgments. Each group was asked to lift a single brass weight varying in weight from 11 grams to 560 grams and to judge each weight on a three-category scale of "light," "medium," or "heavy." Tresselt calculated the average weight of the weights labeled "medium" by both groups. The average weight of the weights felt to be "medium" by the jewelers was 243 grams, whereas the weightlifters judged as "medium" a weight with an average weight of 278. More physical heaviness was required for the more muscular judges to mentally perceive "medium." So background experiences have a distinct effect—what amounts to a biasing effect—on one's perception of lightness or heaviness. Again, such judgment is not "absolute"; it is relative to the background experiences and particularly to the background beliefs of the person making judgments.

Judgments that may at first appear to be different actually follow similar discernment and comparison principles. For instance, if I ask you "Who was the better president, Lincoln or Roosevelt?" your decision is a judgment of two discernible persons along some reference-scale dimension of "Presidential Greatness." But suppose I ask you "Which is heavier, a Ford® or a Chevrolet®?" In this second example, your judgment would be a comparative process, but *in principle* you could come up with an absolutely accurate answer. All you'd have to do is get access to the manufacturers' specifications for each car. But the problem with the first question is that there are no manufacturers' specifications for something as worrisomely subjective as whether Lincoln or Roosevelt was the "better president." The issue of Presidential Greatness is vague, ambiguous, and could potentially be the source of hot arguments and sharp interpersonal disagreements. We do not usually have radical speech and public polarization and divisiveness over judgments of an automobile's weight; that is because we can easily agree on what "weight" is. But when we judge presidents, for example, we are cast into a sea of ambiguities, uncertainties, and personal bias. This is where we get into trouble. You will never get a strong Democrat to say that Ronald Reagan was a great president, and my Republican father would never say that Democrat FDR was a great president. We have our subjective reference scales of Presidential Greatness, but those reference scales operate very differently depending on our party and on our self-identification. As we shall see, we now know why those scales operate so differently.

FOUNDATIONAL RESEARCH THAT REVEALED THE MAIN FEATURES OF JUDGMENT

Our understanding of the many different forms that human judgment takes is based on a solid foundation of over a century of research. It is important that the basic principles of this science now be discussed because they underlie nearly every topic that I discuss from this point on. The critical insight into endorsing processes and radical hearing began in another era, the mid- to late-1800s. In the 1860s, one of the very earliest psychological researchers, Gustav Theodor Fechner, investigated the way we judge the world of stimuli around us. His book *Elements of Psychophysics* is generally regarded as the foundational work in experimental psychology.[2] At that time, psychological science was still a branch of philosophy, so it was natural that there were questions common to both disciplines. One of the fundamental questions linking the two fields sought an answer to "the mind-body problem." What is the relationship between what we receive as stimulation through our five senses (the "body" part of the equation) and our *perceptions,* our mental interpretations of that sensory input (the "mind" part of the question)? Technically, this line of reasoning seeks to answer the question: *What is the psychophysical relationship?* This term is an important one. Note its derivation: "psycho" = mind, and "physics" = physical.

From the very earliest days of psychological science, attention has been focused on understanding how it is that people's sensory and perceptual experiences are "translated" into their mental understanding of their world. The key insight is that the world we live in is both a physical world of weights, sounds, smells, textures, and so on; and a social world of beliefs, attitudes, emotions, and so on. By extending that powerful insight, we now know that we perceive and judge our social world in ways that follow the same basic principles as the ways in which we judge our physical world. We have one mental system for judging the meanings and values of what we perceive. The principles whereby this system operates give us a generalized framework for studying the similarities and differences in the way people respond to their physical world. More importantly, these principles reveal the social world of people's hot-button attitudes and beliefs. It is an amazingly neat fit between our science and the workings of the human mind in its natural physical and social setting.

As you know, science is reductionistic: it attempts to cut through the surface appearances of phenomena and uncover the irreducible core elements and processes that animate the surface reality that we perceive. To do this, it employs techniques to discover basic units and testable processes. Although at first glance this topic may seem a bit distant from what we want to learn about radical hearing, it is important for the issues that will be discussed in coming chapters.

In the realm of our responding to our physical and sensory world, the basic units of perception and judgment are to be found by careful measurement on both sides of the equation. Physical measurement is direct: the experimenter presents some objects of known (measurable) physical properties—size, weight, loudness—to be judged, and then provides the participant with some "response language," which puts their perceptions and responses into a reportable form by giving them easily understood ways to report those feelings. For example, the experimenter can give participants a stimulus whose weight, measured in grams, ounces, pounds, is easily discerned. Or the experimenter can project sounds measured in decibels, or flash lights measured with lumen. Given a particular stimulus, the experimenter then provides appropriate judgment categories for the participants to use to report their sensations. These would be assessed in lay terms such as "heaviness," "loudness," or "brightness." Most typically, though, the participants would be instructed to answer questions using meaningful psychological dimensions, such as "How heavy or light is this stimulus?" or "How soft or loud is this noise?" or "How dim or bright is this stimulus?" These dimensions of perception are easily understood, and people can make judgments without having to be trained to do so: to judge the weight of your Chevrolet, read the manufacturer's manual. The judgments that people give are very stable, and there is a lot of agreement among people as they act as "judges" reporting their sensations. This all seems simple, but such judgment is a highly sophisticated skill that humans (and animals) possess while being remarkably accurate in their judgments. What I mean by "accurate" is the point of experimental research: to determine the exact relationship between the input through the senses and the output in the judgments the person makes.

Literally hundreds of studies have shown that there are quantitative "psychophysical functions" that demonstrate clean mathematical relationships between physical stimulation and psychological perception. Chemistry, physics, and biology get a lot of credit for being "hard-nosed" sciences, but I think that psychophysical science is just as analytical and rigorous in understanding phenomena as the more traditional sciences. Discoveries of psychophysical functions and laws should be eligible for a Nobel Prize in the same way that such discoveries in the so-called harder sciences are. Psychophysical science is even more impressive when we describe the number of modern inventions that are based on its methodology. Even better, this model provides the key insight into how people who adopt radical hearing come to perceive and judge their world; this insight is especially powerful because it reveals how people perceive the beliefs of those with whom they agree and, more importantly, of those with whom they disagree.

So the same logic and virtually the same methods in traditional psychophysical research on sensory processes apply to the judgment processes that are involved when we investigate human communication processes such as those operating in radical hearing. In that case, we would begin with biased opinion statements such as are involved in radical speech. To do this, we would measure opinion statements in terms of how "pro" or "con" the participants feel about a particular topic. We would determine to what extent they are "strongly pro" or "heavily biased against" or "totally favorable" or "bigoted" or "biased" or "extremist" or "anti-American"—any number of such distinctions can be made about opinion statements. These dimensions of judgment are the daily-living equivalent of the experimental psychology laboratory judgments of weight, loudness, brightness, and so on. The upcoming chapters delve into these more complex but more "realistic" uses of psychophysical techniques.

Some of the basic procedures show how investigators work both sides of the psychophysical equation in answering the mind-body research problem. To work on the "body" side, the investigator selects the appropriate scale for judgment, a reference scale. In our simplified version, the case of weight perception, the research participant is provided with small brass weights varying in weight from 30, 40, 50 grams up to 300 to 400 grams or more, depending on the question being investigated. To assess the perception/mental experience side of the equation, the participants are simply asked to report their judgments of what they think about the relevant stimuli. To do this, they are instructed to use a graded scale of judgment categories for each stimulus presentation. So, in the case of weight perception, our cardinal example, the instructor will suggest that the participant use, say, a five-category judgment scale with verbal labels such as "very light," "light," "medium," "heavy," or "very heavy." Often, the participant is simply told to say "1," "2," "3," "4," or "5" for each of their judgments. People can do this fairly easily, and they are very vigilant to make sure that they "get it right." But human language is highly sensitive and provides all sorts of verbal categories for judgments. The same type of scale can be used for brightness ("very dim" to "very bright") or for sounds ("very soft" to "very loud"). Margaret Tresselt's study of weightlifters and jewelers is based directly on these principles.

The same process can be used for judging statements of opinion about, for example, "beliefs about God." Someone can judge a series of statements about presidential beliefs or religious beliefs or patriotic beliefs just as they can with any other array of stimuli, physical or verbal. Some of the statements will be judged as, for example, "very acceptable" or "very objectionable" or "very extremely favorable" on up to "extremely unfavorable." The logic is the same as it is with psychophysical sensory judgment, and the techniques are virtually the same, no matter what the stimulus domain or the response domain. This discovery of "the psychophysical relationship" is one of the premier discoveries of psychological science. It is a fundamental principle of how we experience and judge our world. I will demonstrate this by showing how radical speech is experienced.

Next, I want to describe one of the classic experiments in psychophysics as it is applied to human physical judgment. In spite of its seeming simplicity, there are a lot of things going on in this experiment. It shows all the key components of psychophysical processes that will be useful for my upcoming discussion of the basics of radical hearing. I will give a detailed description of how the experiment was conducted and, particularly, for this first laboratory experiment, I want to provide a careful presentation of its actual results. These results show biases and slants in how we judge our world, and they are directly relevant to understanding the research presented in the rest of this book.

THE PSYCHOPHYSICS STUDY BY SHERIF, TAUB, AND HOVLAND

A clear demonstration of the above-mentioned effect comes from one of the major psychophysics study on judgment scales conducted by Muzafer Sherif, Daniel Taub, and Carl Hovland.[3] Although this study was reductionistic because it studied perceptual and judgmental processes with clear-cut physical stimulus dimensions (in this case, weight in grams), the experimenters later extended their research to judgments of attitude and beliefs, represented by verbal statements of opinion made by people who were highly committed on various hot-button topics. These are the premier studies on radical hearing that we will begin studying in the next chapter and those that follow.

In this psychophysical study using brass weights, the experimenters gave their research participants experience in judging six small brass weights ranging from 55 grams to 141 grams. The participants were asked to use a number scale from "1" to "6" to make their judgments. Here are the basic instructions given to the participants:

> Following the lifting of a weight you are to judge its location on a scale of 1 to 6 inclusive.[4]

The participants went through the original series several times to build up a relatively stable reference scale for making their judgments. Then a second cycle of judgments was presented, but this time a new set of weights was added into the series. These weights were selected by the experimenters to systematically increase in heaviness compared to the original series—from 141 grams to 347 grams. (As was mentioned earlier, judgment involves both "discerning" and "comparing.") With the new weights included, the participants were now to make a *comparative judgment*. They were told to make their judgments in comparison pairs by lifting the new weight first and the original weight second, and judging the second weight by its perceived heaviness. The response scale was the same, and the original weights were judged again, but now their heaviness was to be compared to the new heavier weight. The stable reference scale the investigators built with their original series of weights was in effect the background scenery against which the new action of additional weights was to be judged.

The psychophysical questions being asked were: How are our judgments influenced, if at all, by the presence of new stimuli that are either near to the original series or varying in "distance" in terms of greater and greater amounts of the physical stimulus dimension? What happens when extreme stimuli are experienced? What we are looking for is what happens to middle-range stimuli, for that is where there is uncertainty and ambiguity in making careful discriminations; the end stimuli are much easier to discriminate against and to compare. The logic of this judgment process will apply directly to the discussion in the next chapters, when we will look for those same types of effects when we study judgments of statements of opinion on certain hot-button, emotionally involving statements.

Presented below (figure 3.1) is a visual representation of both the procedures and the results of the study. Each of the separate lines going downward represents a separate experiment, so we can easily see how each of the stimulus conditions compares to the others. The experiments themselves vary in only one way: the weight chosen to be the comparison weight. Note that there are small arrows indicating the weight of the new comparison weights at varying amounts of heaviness, starting with the heaviest weight of the original scale. Note also that on the bottom lines of the new series, its lightest weight was actually the same weight at the (formerly) highest weight in the original series. The averaged judgments of the participants are plotted as bars of frequency of usage of each of the six categories of judgments. Let us go through the data set one line at a time, to see how people respond in this kind of experimental arrangement.

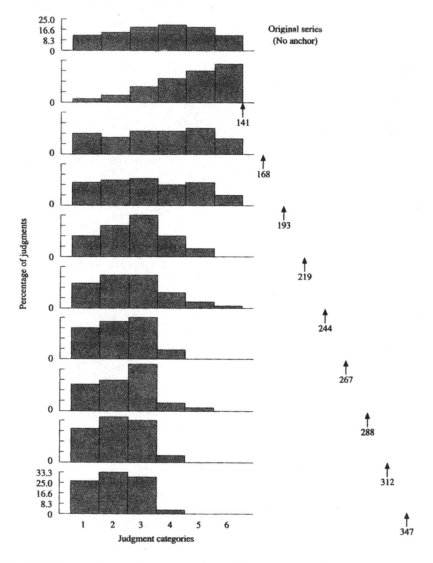

Figure 3.1. Frequencies of category usage for weights with increasingly heavier anchoring weights.[5]

Several fundamental principles of perception and judgment are displayed in this figure. First, note that in the top line of judgments, there is a nearly equal frequency of the use of the six categories of judgment. That would be as expected because the original six weights were deliberately chosen by the experimenters to be equally spaced in actual weight. People's perception of their sensory input mirrors very directly the actual stimulus dimension, in this case, the weight of the stimuli being judged. That is a standard psychophysical effect.

The next line of judgments shows the ratings made when a 141-gram weight was included as a comparison weight; it was judged to be the same weight as the heaviest weight in the original series. Note a detectable increase of "6" (heavy) judgments. This is the assimilation effect. Stimuli similar to an original judgment category get fused into it; the category becomes broader and more inclusive; things become assimilated when they are similar to the original judgment category. The weight is acting as an *anchor* to the reference scale, pulling judgments of similar stimuli toward it.

The third line down shows a change, a "break in function." The 168-gram weight is detectably heavier than the original 141-gram weight, and the effect is to shrink the usage of the judgments of "6." What was originally heaviest is now not perceived as heaviest; it is now becoming lighter by comparison. Going downward as the comparison weights get heavier and heavier, and more and more remote from the top ("6") category of judgment, the original series is judged as lighter and lighter by comparison. When the heaviest of the new heavy scale of weights, 347 grams, is the anchorage in the new series, judgment categories of "5" and "6" are not even perceived; nearly all the original weights are rated "1," "2," or "3," and only a very few are judged as "4." This is a very visual picture of the contrast effect.

In this single study we have seen both contrast and assimilation effects. What varied was the extremity of the new weights (the new anchorages) compared to the existing reference scale. The most significant effect for our purposes is what happens to the middle-range weights; they get shifted around from one pole of the scale toward the other pole, depending on the extremity of the anchorage weights. We will see later that extreme radical statements have the same effect when we are judging what we hear when other people communicate their beliefs to us.

The experiment was conducted a second time with a new set of judgment weights and new anchoring stimulus weights, and five judgment categories, but this time the comparison series was systematically *lighter* than the original series, dropping from 97 grams to a very light 41 grams. The results of this second experiment are displayed in figure 3.2 below.

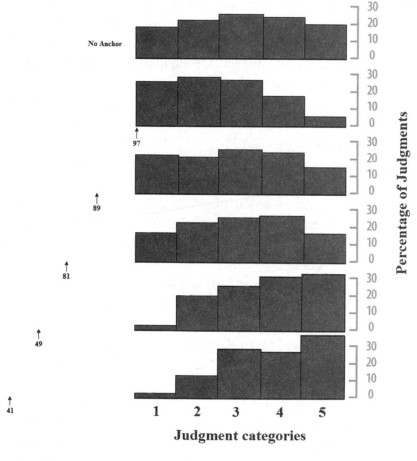

Figure 3.2. Frequencies of category usage for weights with increasingly lighter anchoring weights.[6]

We see that the operation of the assimilation effect with the comparison weight, 75 grams, is closest to the original stimulus series; there is a tendency for a bunching up and increased usage of the lightest judgment category of "1." As the comparison-stimulus weights get lighter and lighter, the use of the heavier categories of judgment increases; the world is getting heavier and heavier when the comparison world is lighter and lighter. Again, this is a demonstration of the contrast effect, as shown in Margaret Tresselt's experiment with her weightlifters and jewelers.

This shifting of the meaning of something due to its judgmental context or reference scale is the key to a psychophysical approach to radical-hearing effects. Let us use the example of the 141-gram weight to demonstrate the chief dynamics of how these judgment principles operate. What happens if the experimenter switches the series of weights to the following series: 141 grams is the lightest, and 347 grams is the heaviest. The key result of this shift in the reference scale is that the 141-gram weight, formerly judged as "very, very heavy," is now called "very, very light." The only thing that has changed is the stimulus series, the "environment," the theater scenery against which the 141-gram weight is experienced. It is exactly the same weight, and the response categories are the same. Since the weight cannot change, it is the perceptual scale that flexes and adjusts to the new world. The psychological meaning of that single brass weight has been dramatically changed by its context; it is either light or heavy depending on its place in a light or heavy environment. If we combine both sets of weights that vary from 55 grams up to the 347-gram weight, then participants will tend to rate the brass weight as "medium."

Well, which is it? Is it "medium," or it is "light," or it is "heavy"? It is all of these, but any one judgment of its properties is completely dependent on the range of other stimuli in which it is embedded, and the key to that is the total range of other weights in the series. Judgment is, therefore, not absolute; it is not purely mental or purely physical; it is *contextual*. The introduction of lighter or heavier weights shifts the perspectives for making judgments in a context of a wider or narrower range of categories for judging the stimuli.

This kind of research shows that our experiencing of our physical world is actually much more than just sensory stimulation; our mental experiences are more than our sensory experiences, and we can use sensory processes to demonstrate that effect. For example, when we judge the weight of a stimulus on some response scale, our judgment is more than just the stimulus property itself. Our judgment brings into play our mental experiences and all that that implies.

However, there are some important subtleties in how this process of making judgments and decisions operates. This effect was demonstrated by Donald Brown in his psychophysical study, "Stimulus-Similarity and the Anchoring of Subjective Scales."[7] Brown used classical psychophysical weight-lifting procedures, but he added a very clever and very revealing innovation. He used a wooden tray to present the brass-weight stimuli to the participants. In one of the conditions, the experimenter asked participants to move the tray to the other side of the table. Now, the wooden tray's weight was carefully calibrated to be exactly the same weight as some of the heavier weights that the participants were instructed to judge in terms of their heaviness. If our experiences were totally sensory and based on just the physical properties of stimuli, then lifting the tray should have had the same effect on the judgment of the weights as did the actual stimulus weight; lifting the tray should have skewed the perception of the lighter weights to being even lighter. But that is not what happened. Instead, there was almost no effect at all on the judgments of the weights. It was as if the participants had not even lifted the tray. So there has to be some experience of meaningful connection between a given stimulus and the context in which the judgments are occurring. We have to go beyond the physical to make sense of the disconnect demonstrated by these results. The weights fit the task, but the wooden tray did not, so the key is the meaning the participant attaches to the judgment task. To quote Brown, "Since they did not think of it as a weight, it had no effect."[8] Their judgments, therefore, cannot be thought of as purely sensory. Our minds may receive physical stimulation, but they do not process information in strictly physical terms. That is why we have the term *psychophysical.* Brown's study clearly shows that the processing is "psycho-logical" in addition to being physical.

We know these results are reliable because they have been repeated in a similar psychophysical experiment conducted by Donald Johnson.[9] Studying category judgments of weights, Johnson had his participants engage in multiple judging tasks with varying sizes of weights. However, he noted one interesting aspect of those multiple exposures to the weights. According to Johnson, "During rest pauses the Ss [subjects] would often move a chair or lift a book without apparent effect upon their scales of value based on lifting the stimulus weights . . . knowledge of such conditions would contribute to psychological understanding of relevance, an almost untouched problem in the psychology of judgment."[10]

Chairs and books weigh a lot more than the brass weights used in psychology experiments, but unless they are somehow perceived as meaningfully relevant, then they are simply dissociated from the judging experience. Both of these studies set the stage for moving research on the psychology of judgment out of the realm of simple sensory processing and into the world of psychological meaning— the world of "relevance," as Johnson called it. Even more important, though, is that there are emotional factors as well as "relevance" that can be detected by psychophysical methods. The principles are the same, and I will discuss a number of judgment studies that target a high level of cognitive and emotional processes that I propose underlay hot-button judgmental processes.

In later chapters, I will show that one's personal values, one's very concept of his or her own self, set the context by which radical speech is "discerned" and "compared" by rendering some final judgment to either endorse the statement and accept it as one's own or to reject it and not allow it into one's personal set of beliefs and values. People who are highly emotionally involved experience a narrowing of their sense of perspective. They find as acceptable to their belief systems only a highly selected and narrow range of statements, and they reject most other statements as unacceptable. That is what Winston Churchill described as one problem with fanatics; they cannot change the topic because they do not see any viable alternatives to their points of view. So the total set of the "meaning" of the stimulus itself and the person's background of experience and values set the context for judgment. In radical hearing, these become distorted and biased by high emotional involvement.

PSYCHOPHYSICAL RELATIONSHIPS IN THE REAL WORLD

Assessing mind–body relationships has turned out to be much more than an ivory-tower pursuit. Businesses that develop consumer products are well aware of this science. In fact, businesses employ psychophysicists, sensory psychologists, and engineers to help them develop products using the best scientific evidence. When cosmetics manufacturers want to develop and market a new brand of lipstick, they perform psychophysical tests on chemical compounds, varying the thickness, texture, smoothness, color, and fragrance of their test compounds, and then test them out on actual consumers (preference test panels). Basically, they ask the consumer judges to rate the lipstick samples on such qualities as "smoothness," with scales such as "very hard" to "neutral" to "very smooth" or some such dimension. They eventually ask questions like "How desirable is this lipstick to you?" on a scale of "not desirable at all" to "questionable" to "very desirable." Such steps in product development are critical to many industries and forms of products. Billions of dollars of sales hinge on this product-development process. The same principles of judgments of pleasantness and desirability (or unpleasantness and rejection) apply to products, for example, the recognizable "new car smell," the sound of a car door slamming, the powerful feeling of the steering wheel, the acceleration of the motor, and so on. The taste of new foods, the flavor of new sodas, the sound transmitted by hearing aids, the design of airplane cockpit instrument panels, the visual display of air traffic–controller screens. The list is nearly endless. It all depends on the product and the rating scale that the developers think are most important to their marketing plans. In fact, psychophysicists have engineered much of the daily life we lead, and much of that is based on our use of the psychophysical principles of how people experience and react to their world. And you can see how flexible the psychophysical methods are: just find the connection between the product properties and the physical dimensions that are thought to be the most critical ones for product desirability.

These ideas help illuminate the experiences we have in our own daily living. For instance, on an extremely cold day, can you tell whether it is 1 degree or 2 degrees or –5 degrees? Typically, we would use a broad term, like "bitterly cold" or some such description. As a personal example, I live Phoenix, Arizona, which is at the northern edge of the Sonoran Desert. In the hottest part of the summer, I have trouble telling if a midafternoon temperature of 114 degrees is actually 112 or 113 or 115 or 116. They are all HOT, and I cannot tell the difference. Ditto for Alaska in the winter. Readings all around the lowest or the highest point of the scale all get judged and assimilated into the lowest- or highest-end category. When we experience any kind of new stimuli, we don't have the ability to make categorical distinctions because differences at the extreme cannot be detected. Similarly, and to choose a pretty likely example, a strong Democrat would judge as "a good Democrat" anyone with a wide range of behaviors as long as that person is labeled as a "Democrat." More tellingly, such a person will likely judge as acceptable some pretty wild types of political shenanigans as long as they come from a "Democrat." To be fair, Republicans also tolerate seemingly extreme behaviors from other politicians as long as they carry the label "Republican." It scarcely needs mentioning that neither party would remotely accept those same behaviors from someone in the opposing party. I will have a great deal more to say about this assimilation effect in later chapters.

However, research shows that assimilation does not go on infinitely and that reference scales cannot be stretched beyond a particular point. It turns out that as the new, more extreme stimuli are experienced, as new events are more and more extreme, then a sudden shift occurs, and the perceptions shift *away* from the new anchorage judgments in an opposite direction. There is a break in function: the contrast effect. In our simple brass weights example, a "heavy" judgment of one of the heavy weights will suddenly change to a "lighter" judgment if you pick up an even heavier weight. A woman may be considered "good-looking," but compared to a stunningly beautiful model, she may, unfortunately, be judged as "less good-looking." American social critics are up in arms about the saturation of our media with extremely thin (but beautiful, of course) models in gorgeous clothing; the average woman looks less good in this judgmental frame of reference. Similarly, most men—even those in excellent physical shape—will look pretty puny compared to Arnold Schwarzenegger in his prime.

I can make an even more vivid point. My colleagues Douglas Kenrick and Sara Gutierres demonstrated the "anchor effect" on judgment standards of beauty in a study of college students.[11] This effect is also known as the "Farrah Fawcett Effect," and you will soon see why. The study investigated the consequences on male college students' judgments of the attractiveness of college women. The judgment itself was simple: How attractive did the male students find a picture of a college-age woman when they were shown it under the guise of her suitability as a date? Approached in their college dormitories' TV rooms, the students were told that the experimenters had a friend visiting town, and they were trying to find out if they should try to "set him up" with a date, whose picture they had brought with them. The men were asked to judge the picture quickly and spontaneously on a 7-point scale, with "1" meaning "very unattractive, "4" meaning "exactly average," and "7" meaning "very attractive." They made their judgments, and the experimenters moved on to another dorm TV room, presumably gathering more judgments on the photo so their friend could get a good sample that would help him decide whether or not to date the woman.

Unbeknownst to the students, the picture had previously been embedded in a large sample of other pictures of females that had been used as stimuli for a judgment task using other groups of student judges. Those pictures varied in levels of attractiveness, and the experimenters picked one from the middle range of attractiveness (4.1 on a 7-point scale, to be exact).

So, armed with this stimulus with a known scale value, the experimenters then carried out their key manipulation of the experiment. They altered the anchoring stimuli for the judgments of the students in the TV room by changing the *timing* of the experiment. The students were approached during one of two close but importantly different times of the evening. The timing was determined by the wildly popular television show *Charlie's Angels.* This high-energy series showcased three female crime fighters involved in various exciting scenarios, but the show was mostly famous for the amazing beauty of its main characters, one of whom was Farrah Fawcett.

In one group, the control "no-anchor" condition, the students were asked to make their judgments just *before* the broadcast of the show. Presumably the males had come to the TV room to bathe themselves in the beauty and titillation of those stunning women, but the show had not yet started when they were asked to make their judgments. The experimental condition (the "anchor" condition) was conducted in exactly the same way as the control condition, but the students were asked to make their judgments immediately *after* watching the show. So, the control group had not yet seen the lovely Farrah Fawcett and the other Angels, and the experimental subjects had just seen them. The latter group had just been exposed to an hours' worth of what we call here an *extreme anchor,* while the control group had not yet been exposed to those beautiful extreme anchors.

The results of the study were exactly what would be predicted by a contrast effect. The control group who had not yet seen *Charlie's Angels* rated the average female's picture as 4.0, nearly the same as the score the experimenters had determined for the picture based on the earlier independent sample of students, but the students who had just watched *Charlie's Angels* rated the picture as 3.4, more than half a unit down toward "less attractive," a notable decrease in perceived beauty. The title of the Kenrick–Gutierres research report is "Contrast Effects and Judgments of Physical Attractiveness: When Beauty Becomes a Social Problem." Now that you know how extreme anchors can bias our perceptions and our judgment processes, perhaps the title makes a lot of sense. Kenrick and Gutierres cleverly saw the beautiful Farrah Fawcett as likely to act as such an anchor. By running the experiment in a natural environment and using the all-pervasive medium of TV as the experimental setting, they neatly linked our daily judgment processes with the solid foundation of psychophysical research theory and method.

We are seeing this "problem" played out in contemporary society. A number of social commentators are concerned that modern women are being held to excessively high standards of beauty. They worry that such concerns over appearance and problems with weight maintenance are of near-epidemic proportions. These concerns seem to be correlated with intense media attention given to New York fashion models and beautiful Hollywood stars. There seems to be less concern with women holding men to similar standards, although, presumably, the same principles should apply.

ASSIMILATION AND CONTRAST IN EXTREMIST SPEECH

Radical or extremist statements can create the same types of effects as discussed above. That is, assimilation and contrast effects in judgment explain a great deal of what happens when people are exposed to extreme speech. In a more emotional type of judgment, if a person has "love of Christianity" on their reference scale and would accept as a personal belief the statement "Christianity is the best hope for the future of the world," then that person is much more likely to vote for political candidate X if the candidate is a Christian. That characteristic of the candidate will be judged toward the end point of the scale, naturally at the positive end of the scale. That same candidate is not as likely to get the vote of someone who does not believe that statement about Christianity. In fact, people who believe the extreme opposite of the statement would most likely reject the strongly pro-Christian politician.

This assimilation effect is much more than an interesting laboratory phenomenon. Assimilation effects may well be key components to the prejudice and stereotyping that arise in social relations and intergroup conflict. In American history, for instance, if someone was labeled a communist sympathizer ("comsymp"), that person was often thought of as a "commie"—no suffix. At one time, the term *pinko* denoted the equivalent of being a "godless atheistic communist." In recent American history, being sympathetic to the Socialist Party might have resulted in being labeled a "communist." In racial relations, a dark-skinned person is often referred to as being "black." The offspring of anyone with dark-skinned ancestors is considered to be "black," down through the generations, apparently forever. The Nazi government traced lineages of its citizens back many generations, searching for "Jewishness," usually with lethal consequences. After the events of 9/11, a young to middle-age male who is Arabic in appearance (dark skin, a beard), might be considered by the average American to be a "terrorist." Undocumented workers raise similar anxieties. Important distinctions among people are not being made because of the biased judgment scales that people engage when they are dealing with emotional feelings.

This point can be expressed visually. In the earlier part of this chapter, I developed the analogy of theater scenery that sets the background for understanding the context that people bring to a judgment situation. I noted that our own personal background experiences set the context for our judgments, and that those experiences can be more or less physical, or they can be psychological. But no matter what, they can be compelling, even if you tried to eliminate or ignore them, even if you are told to ignore them. For instance, look at the figure below. Every basic psychology textbook for the past fifty years has displayed this figure, so we are dealing with standard principles here:

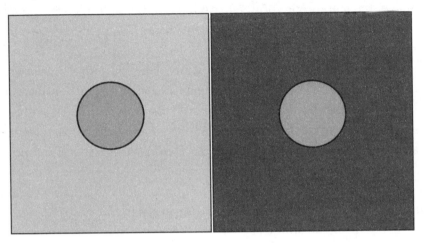

Figure 3.3. Visual contrast effect.

Look carefully at the two circles. Note that the one on the left looks darker than the one on the right. It seems so obviously clear that the circles are different colors. But in fact they are not different; they are *exactly the same* circle! I promise you. What is different between the two panels is the background. One is darker than the other, and that darker tone makes the circle, *by contrast,* appear lighter. Even once you know this, the contrast effect is so compelling that your conscious process has great difficulty in denying it.

When someone hears and personally adopts what a speaker is saying, their judgment of the intention of that message is invariably colored by the hearer's own background of attitudes and beliefs. If these attitudes and beliefs are moderate, or centrist, the person's judgment of the meaning of the speech will be milder than if the person's background is extreme. That is how hearing radical speech and engaging radical hearing affects us: they "color" our mental backgrounds and lead us to distortions and to perceiving things in ways that are not true. Again, I assure you that those circles are the same shade.

As you can guess, in the realm of radical hearing, when we are dealing with extremist statements of belief and opinion, extremist statements will force moderate, middle-of-the-road statements to the opposite end of the scale. What might be judged as a moderate statement by unbiased observers can, in the hands of an extremist, become supportive of "the enemy opinion." No wonder that "voices of moderation can't be heard."

There are many examples in chapters 1 and 2 of what an end-anchor statement of opinion looks like, but to refresh our memories of how extremist statements can anchor a judgment scale, we have this colorful example from Rev. Pat Robertson: "The feminist agenda is not about equal rights for women. It is about a socialist antifamily political movement that encourages women to leave their husbands, kill their children, practice witchcraft, destroy capitalism, and become lesbians."[12]

A moderate statement cannot stand up to this sort of extreme statement. Suppose I ask you to tell me how "pro" or "anti" you are regarding the statement "Planned parenthood provides many services for women." Most moderate, uncommitted people would judge this statement as either dead-center neutral or at least moderate. But someone like Pat Robertson would likely judge it as a statement intended to say positive things about Planned Parenthood. For such a person, the judged position of the statement would be pushed farther away from the middle of the scale; in this case to the "pro" end of the scale. When compared to extreme anchor stimuli on the scale, the voice of moderation can get lost. Middle-of-the-road speech will not be perceived as "middle" in the face of such extreme statements. And it does not take explicit instructions from an experimenter to make the comparison; it happens automatically. As I said earlier, *all judgment is comparative,* and all too often our attitudes and emotions are the comparison points when we judge someone else's beliefs and opinions.

These two kinds of end-point anchoring effects, assimilation and contrast, have the consequence of setting the outer boundaries of one's judgment scale. In radical hearing, extreme speech has the effect of establishing end points of a person's reference scale. Endorsing radical speech will enhance assimilation processes, and so somewhat related people and ideas will more easily fall into the end-point categories because of anchoring effects. This interpretation of social conflict's prevalent stereotyping and prejudice is speculative, but it is consistent with what is known of how judgment effects operate under conditions of high emotions and biases, especially when there is social conflict.

POLITICS AND POLITICIANS: USING JUDGMENT PRINCIPLES FOR STRATEGIC SELF-PRESENTATION

Our daily lives are infused with assimilation and contrast principles. For instance, if an unknown politician wants to run for office, an important issue is how to be judged as being in the top rank of the political party, which means how to get assimilated into the top end of the political dimension of the party's judgment scale. Those aspiring to favorable judgments want to be a "10" on the scale. A strong candidate does not want to be judged as a "middle-of-the-road" Democrat or Republican. The candidate has to take stances that are the "heaviest" or "brightest" or "loudest" (to make an analogy with sensory dimensions of judgment) to get *assimilated* into the most desirable category and to be thought of as part of it. In addition, the candidate hopes his or her opponent will be regarded as "off-the-scale right-wing" or "off-the-scale left-wing" and thus will be contrasted away from the acceptable category. Candidates try to get their opponents to be perceived as *beyond* that party's judgment scale, to be seen as being so radical as to be undesirable and thus contrasted away from the desirable ends of that reference scale. While a fanatic speaker would be expected to loudly proclaim one narrow perspective, people who *hear* that speech do not necessarily have to apply the same narrow perspective. If they reject its narrowness and avoid "getting" the emotional contamination from radical speech, then there may be a chance to undermine the damaging effects of radical hearing's distortion of a person's sense of perspective about the issue. Radical, highly negative emotions tend to narrow one's perspective and scale of judgment. In effect, when a person's thinking and judgment become dominated by assimilation and contrast effects, that person has, in a very real sense, lost his or her sense of perspective. That is where our current social divisiveness and polarized thinking gets its hold on how we think and respond to each other. In the next chapter, I explain in more detail why it is in our very self-concepts, the beliefs of who we are, that we will find the main cause of our civic discourse.

CHAPTER 4

EMOTIONS, ATTITUDES, AND JUDGMENT PROCESSES

It should be clear by now that nearly everything I have said about hearing processes, radical or moderate, has been *rational*, cool, and cognitive. That is because the science of psychophysics is just that: rational. It deals with people's rational judgments about, for example, whether a given stimulus is a "3" or a "6," or if it is physically "heavier" or "lighter" than a comparison stimulus. This is a good model to follow when we talk about the physical world, and it provides good insights into the "discern" and "compare" components of the judgment process. After all, we want our airplane pilots to make cool and correct decisions about distance between the plane and the ground; we want our police to make smart decisions about speed limits and traffic; and we certainly want our physicians to be rational when it comes to prescribing medications or recommending surgery. These are all *comparative* decisions in which the judge's task is to discern correctly among the alternatives that are present in the stimulus series. Discerning and comparing are key components of our definition of *judgment* that was discussed in chapter 3. In fact, entire industries are based on valid and accurate discerning and comparing among different alternatives. This rational model of human thinking and judgment is a valuable one; science needs to follow this model, and, ideally, industry, government, and the general public also would do well to follow it.

However, human history shows that rational models of thinking processes are not very good predictors of how people actually behave. This redirecting of our thinking is especially needed when we are dealing with more subjective aspects of the stimulus world when it is not so clearly based on measurable physical dimensions. The recent popularity of behavioral economics is based on the breaking down of the once-dominant model of "rational man." Human history is filled with examples of rational thinking gone wrong. Radical speech and radical hearing have a lot to do with these failures. Can the psycho-physical approach be used to understand and to perhaps avoid these disasters?

THE SUBJECTIVE AND EMOTIONAL SIDE OF OUR LIVES

The missing ingredient in many cases is the *emotional* component of human functioning. Many of our decisions are influenced either by what we want to happen or what we do not want to happen. We are wired to have emotional reactions before we are even aware of our rational considerations. Interestingly, this same dominance by emotional processes guides the lives of animals as well; they seek out what they want, and they avoid things that might harm them. This is what Robert Zajonc meant when he said that "affect is primary": emotions are the first step in much of our information processing. Zajonc has shown that events that trigger emotional feelings such as liking and disliking have effects on our judgment and decision processes *prior to* our ever becoming consciously aware of those events. Stimuli that signal an emotional reaction actually bypass the frontal ("thinking") lobes of the brain, operating independently of our conscious mental processing and tapping into emotional areas of the brain. Often we have judged something without even knowing we have judged it. Some psychologists argue that much of our mental life occurs after all the interesting internal emotional reactions have already occurred, and we just find ways to rationalize and explain what we have already unconsciously "decided." Even a brief chat with someone will quickly reveal what that person values in life. You will soon hear the negative things that are on that person's mind: anger, aggression, hostility. But, on the positive side, you also will hear the love, devotion, and optimism. These emotional concerns dominate what people think and how they lead their lives. We wear our emotions on our sleeves, and as Scottish philosopher David Hume said, "Reason is, and ought only to be the slave of the passions, and can never pretend to any other office than to serve and obey them."[1]

This, of course, is what happens when people endorse radical speech. As a consequence, radical hearing carries with it a major component of "prior emotional reactions," and conscious thinking and reasoning follow *after* the emotional reactions occur. This is what is meant by the word *prejudice*, literally, a prejudgment. People can have a prejudice about anything (because they can judge anything), but the term refers specifically to the emotional feelings one brings to a judgment situation. A personal story: When I was much younger, in my household there were three alphabet letters that one dared not link together into a phrase. The letters? *F*, *D*, and *R*. Saying those letters got my father into an instant lather. He hated the New Deal because some of its policies sent federal agents into rural areas to carry out drastic actions to control prices, and Franklin Delano Roosevelt was head of the government that instituted those policies. My father's lifelong endorsement of Republican politics never wavered during the course of my growing up. It was a situation of prejudgment, pure and simple.

So how can psychophysical science come to grips with these kinds of emotional biasing effects? As a first-pass idea, it seems pretty clear that the participants in the above-mentioned weight-lifting studies do not really *care* about those brass weights. They could care less if the weight is being well treated and humanely cared for by the experimenter. It is a safe bet that their emotions, such as liking and disliking, did not color their discernment and comparison processes as they followed the experimenter's instructions. In fact, if they had felt some emotional commitments, the experimenters would have eliminated their responses from the data, as such feelings might make the results unreliable. But attitudes functioning as feelings of like or dislike are one of the chief sources of bias in studies of reference-scale effects, as I shall soon show.

HOW ATTITUDES AND OPINIONS REFLECT UNDERLYING JUDGMENT PROCESSES

What people say about what they believe is most commonly expressed in their attitudes and opinions. The concept of *attitude* is probably the most important one in the social sciences. A good summarizing of the various definitions commonly used by researchers is the following statement:

> Attitude (noun): A disposition or a tendency to respond positively or negatively toward a certain idea, object, person, or action.

The key point of this definition is that an attitude is a predisposition, a preset tendency to respond in either a positive or a negative way to something. Researchers characterize attitudes as having (1) a direction—positive or negative, "pro" or "con," favorable or unfavorable, and so on, and (2) an intensity gradient from weak to strong. Generally, weak attitudes are more commonly defined as opinions and are more changeable and variable. But a strong attitude is considered to be hard-line, rigid, inflexible, and radical. A highly patriotic American might *dislike* "Socialism" because he *really hates* "Communism" and fails to note that there are important differences between the two. Someone feeling so much hate that they ignore what are in fact quite important distinctions is a key indicator of bias. Accurately assessing someone's attitude is a major part of being able to understand and predict their behavior. You know pretty well how a radical speaker is going to react to something when you know that person's attitude. That is what attitudes do: they give a person a way to interpret and make sense of their world, while the rest of us may not be so enthralled with their single-track mind.

There is a good deal of useful information about radical hearing among the large body of research on attitudes. I will review some of that research next.

THE BREAKTHROUGH IN ATTITUDE MEASUREMENT

National attitude and opinion survey companies have developed highly sophisticated techniques for surveying the public's attitudes. They are good at what they do, and they sell their information for good money. Their work is impressive: they can make spot-on predictions about elections, business trends, and consumer preferences, for example. This is good science, too, in that these types of surveys are based on hard-evidence research methods.

The earliest insight on how to scientifically assess attitudes was pioneered by one of the greatest figures in the psychological sciences: Louis Leon Thurstone. The Psychometrics Laboratory he founded at the University of North Carolina in the early 1930s is considered an impressive national resource to this day. His landmark work in psychometrics is outlined in his book coauthored with E. J. Chave, *The Measurement of Attitude.*[2] In this work, he developed the concept of a *rating scale* for assessing beliefs and attitudes. Thurstone and Chave's insight came with their assumption that opinions and attitudes about *social* entities could be judged on reference scales. They were fully familiar with psychophysical judgment techniques, but their innovation was to move from judging the perceived physical properties of objects (small brass weights, loudness of tones, brightness of lights, and so on) to more verbally based rating scales of written statements. In this area, they pioneered the basic method for their extension of psychophysical procedures into the domain of investigating attitudes and emotions regarding touchy social issues.

They chose religious beliefs as their topic, specifically developing their scale titled "List of Opinions about the Church." Not many issues are more emotion-laden and heated than belief or disbelief in God. Attending church or temple and related activities are the pivots for deep personal relationships for many people. And wars and hatred related to religion have been and continue to be one of the major causes of social strife. The discussion of religion can be complex, though, because it has also been a major force for altruism and helpfulness, as well as a source of comfort for many. In the following section, I will look at topics more emotionally charged than any physical judgments. This initiates us into the basics of radical speech, so be warned: I will be discussing some touchy issues and sensitive topics. Starting with attitudes toward the church is an appropriate beginning.

It will be helpful for later discussion if I first look briefly at the details of how Thurstone and Chave founded a standard methodology for opinion and attitude surveying in their "List of Opinions about the Church." Note that the word *church*, as it's used by the authors and by me, refers to "church" in general and does not address any specific faith.

To begin their study, Thurstone and Chave obtained a large number of verbal statements about church and religious beliefs from both people and church publications. They then winnowed these down to a final set of 130 statements that covered the entire range of statements of opinion: from very favorable assertions about the church, to neutral statements, to very unfavorable assertions. This was the equivalent of a psychophysics experiment in which the stimulus range for judgment would move, for example, from a very light weight to a very heavy weight. In principle, reference scales can go from zero to, theoretically, limitlessly extremist. So, in the realm of religious beliefs, the scales could range from extreme religiosity to extreme agnosticism and atheism. In extending psychophysical methods to psychosocial methods, then, the idea is to make sure that the stimulus domain—in this case, statements of opinion—covers the range from the most positive response possible to the most negative.

Below are a few of the statements made about "the Church," which were included in Thurstone and Chave's study.

> I have seen no value in the church.
> I believe that membership in a good church increases one's self-respect and usefulness.
> I believe that the church is petty, always quarreling over matters that have no interest or importance.

I believe the church provides most of the leaders for every movement for social welfare.

I think the organized church is an enemy of science and truth.

I find the services of the church both restful and inspiring.

I think the church is a divine institution and deserves the highest respect and loyalty.

I think the church is necessary but it puts its emphasis on the wrong things.

The church is to me primarily a place to commune with God.

I believe that the church is a parasite on society.[3]

The statements were typed onto individual slips of paper, put into one stack, and presented to the research participants. Thurstone and Chave canvassed the Chicago area for volunteers to participate in their project. They administered stacks to a sample of three hundred adults in Chicago, divided into groups. Each group was given instructions to sort the set of 130 statements in the following manner (the instructions below were excerpted directly from the original report):

1. The 130 slips contain statements regarding the value of the church. These have been made by various persons, students, and others.

2. As a first step in the making of a scale that may be used in a test of opinion relation to the church and religion, we want a number of persons to sort these 130 slips into 11 piles.

3. You are given eleven slips with letters on them, A, B, C, D, E, F, G, H, I, J, K. Please arrange these before you in regular order. On slip A put those statements which you believe express the highest appreciation of the value of the church. On slip F put those expressing a neutral position. On slip K put those slips which express the strongest depreciation of the church. On the rest of the slips arrange statements in accordance with the degree of appreciation or depreciation expressed in them.

4. This means that when you are through sorting you will have eleven piles arranged in order of value-estimate from A, the highest, to K, the lowest.[4]

Note that participants were told not to let their own opinions bias their judgments; they were not asked anything about their own opinions; they were instructed simply to categorize each statement according to its degree of "appreciation" or "depreciation" of the church. The scale values and the judgment process itself are essentially equivalent to the "very light" or "medium" or "very heavy" judgments made about brass weights in a traditional psychophysical study. Using letters of the alphabet was a clever innovation. It removed the sense of size or quantity associated with the numerical scale while encouraging judgments of differentness among the various statements of opinion. Such "detection of differences" is more technically called *discrimination*, a term close in meaning to the "discern" part of our definition of *judgment*. I will use this when I discuss radical hearing more explicitly.

With all the statements sorted by the participants, Thurstone and Chave then took each statement and calculated the numerical average of the judgments received from the participants, converting the "A" through "K" judgments into the number system of "1" through "11." Through this process, we now have our "stimuli" measured just as if they were brass weights, but, rather than grams, the numbers represent shades of opinion, from "very favorable" to "very unfavorable," or from "appreciation" to "depreciation," as Thurstone and Chave described the scale. So now we can *quantitatively* build a judgment scale categorizing the opinions represented in the domain of religious beliefs and opinions. For instance, if we say that the first statement on the list of sample responses, "I have seen no value in the church," is 9.9, we know exactly how negative that statement is. The statement "I think the church is a divine institution and deserves the highest respect and loyalty" is rated as 0.2, so we know how extremely favorable it is. The statement "I think the church is necessary but it puts its emphasis on the wrong things" is rated as 5.3, more neutral than either of the other two statements but still slightly negative. Being able to quantitatively measure a "slightly negative" shade of opinion was a major advancement in psychological science. As we shall see, it is in such shading and subtlety of how attitudes and beliefs influence the judgment process that the destructive effects of radical speech become revealed. This is the main theme of the upcoming chapters.

You can see how these statements could be judged (discerned and compared) against someone's personal reference scale. Keep in mind that this group of judges was simply asked to rate each of the statements about how "pro" or "con" they were regarding the church, and no more. This kind of task is virtually a study in the English language: the extent to which these words reflect value judgments about the topic, the church; and adequate language skills are pretty much all this phase of the experiment requires.

The next, and very important, phase of the experiment was to deliberately bring people's opinions about the statements into the judgment process. To complete this phase, Thurstone and Chave recruited a large sample of twelve hundred University of Chicago volunteer research participants. They were simply asked to judge each statement according to how much he or she wanted to *endorse* it; in other words, which statements personally represented their own feelings. The instructions to the participants were as follows:

This is an experimental study of the distribution of attitude toward the church. You will be asked to read a list of statements about the church, and to indorse [*sic*] those that express your own sentiment. Let your own experiences with churches determine your indorsements [*sic*].

Check (✓) every statement below that expresses your sentiment toward the church. Interpret the statements in accordance with your own experiences with churches.[5]

This was the first systematic study of the endorsement process, and it opened up an entirely new way of revealing the fundamental principles of the biases that underpin the radical-hearing process. Some of the questions asked of the participants, among other questions, if they attended church frequently and if they were an active member of a church. The participants were also asked to put a mark on a line representing their attitudes from "Strongly favorable to the church" to "Strongly against the church." These latter questions were intended to provide some direct measure of the person's self-identification about the church. Having this information is the key to checking the validity of the entire procedure, for it allows us to view the responses of subgroups of participants. These subgroups represent the study of opinions that people could hold on the issue of belief in the church.

The results of these analyses provided strong support for the technique to measure attitudes. First, in the graph below, taken directly from the report, we see bar graphs representing the proportions of judgments of endorsements across the total range or scores (the bottom line, from 0 through 11).

The proportions, of course, can vary from 0 percent of the participants' endorsement to 100 percent at any one favorable or unfavorable opinion category on the scale. Of the two graphs, the top one represents participants who said that they *did not* attend church frequently, and the bottom graph represents those who reported that they *did* attend regularly.

The graphs of the proportions show, as might be expected, wide variations in endorsements across the attitude scale. The nonfrequent attendees had a high proportion of their endorsed statements at the unfavorable ("depreciation") end of the scale, while those who attended frequently tended to endorse statements at the favorable ("appreciation") end of the scale. Frequent churchgoers accepted the prochurch statements, and nonfrequent churchgoers accepted the antichurch statements. In the language of test-construction techniques, such findings support what is called the *validity* of the scale: it is clearly measuring what it was designed to measure.

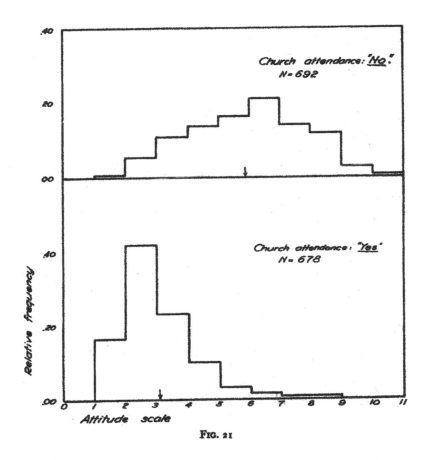

Figure 4.1. Frequency of endorsements of statements of opinions about the church reported by frequent church attendees and nonfrequent church attendees.[6]

It is possible that church attendance alone might not be a totally valid measure of opinions about the church; it might instead reflect some more transient or temporary response, "pro" or "con," to a particular church-related opinion or rejection of such opinion. But actual membership is likely to be a more stable measure of commitment (or, conversely, a rejection of any type of church-related commitment). Thurstone and Chave reanalyzed the data using church membership as the criterion for attitudes. The results are displayed below in figure 4.2.

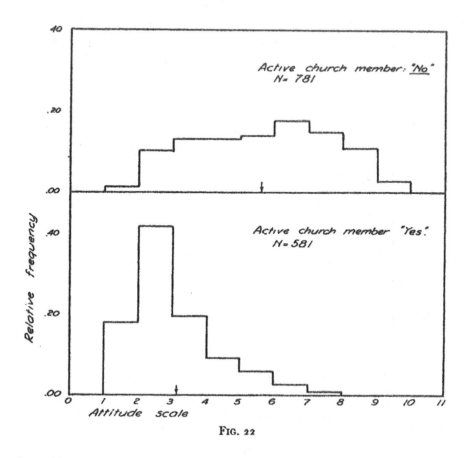

FIG. 22

Figure 4.2. Frequency of endorsements of statements of opinions about the church reported by participants who are active church members and participants who are not active church members.[7]

As is quite clear, both graphs are equally compelling in showing judgmental differences between groups that are so different in terms of actual commitment. The results mirror the results in the previous figure, again reflecting validity of the scale.

Remember that both groups read and judged exactly the same statements; the "stimulus continuum" of eleven possible shades of opinion was identical for both groups, and so the methods were objectively the same for both groups. The only factor that could create a difference between the groups was the emotional commitment of the participants. The results showed that appreciation/depreciation judgments were the opposite of each other because the participants' opinions were on opposite ends of the judgment scale.

Clearly, then, emotional commitments both for churchgoing and against churchgoing had visible effects on what should have been "merely" cognitive judgments. Judging the statements involved more than just simple rational decisions. I cannot conclusively say if one group "distorted" its judgments more than the other, but I can say that both groups showed a slant or bias in the way they regarded the statements. This study has revealed that commitment to or rejection of the values of the church play an important role in judging attitude-relevant statements. It seems unlikely that these same two groups of participants would have judged brass weights any differently: a person presumably would not "appreciate" one particular piece of brass and "depreciate" another one. It might seem a bit silly to make this comparison, but it does raise an interesting question about the extent to which something like a major emotional commitment such as going to church—and consequently endorsing positive church-related statements—might extend to non-church-related issues, even to something like brass weights. That study would be well worth doing.

If churchgoing is an indicator of emotional commitment, the logical issue for investigation is the extent to which emotional commitments can bias judgments about statements *even if* participants are asked to avoid letting their own feelings bias their judgments. Can a person of known commitment, someone who we know has hot-button emotions about a particular issue, respond in the same way as someone who has a commitment to the opposite side of the issue? Furthermore, what kinds of judgment processes can we expect to see from someone who is strongly committed on one side of an issue compared to someone who has an opposite feeling about that issue—or from someone who has no particular opinion on the topic? This question allows us to investigate both "pro" and "con" attitudes and then compare them against the attitudes of someone who has no particular opinion one way or the other. As I will show repeatedly, it is emotional commitment to extreme positions that is the core component of the kinds of judgmental distortions that characterize radical hearing.

A STANDARD FOR ALL SCALE DEVELOPMENT AND TESTING

This careful set of procedures established by Thurstone and Chave has become a gold standard in terms of attitude and opinion measurement. The study of opinions about the church was only an example of proof of a concept; it did not reflect any particular personal bias toward the church or religious sentiments on the part of Thurstone and Chave.

In the decades following Thurstone and Chave's work, a number of social attitudes were opened to investigation. In their book *Scales for the Measurement of Attitudes*, researchers Marvin Shaw and Jack Wright compiled a volume organizing the types of scales into groups of similar topics.[8] They reprinted the actual scales themselves, providing in effect a workbook for social-science research on virtually any topic of interest to investigators and public officials. The reader is encouraged to find this book and look over the impressive range of important social topics and the ways in which the items are arranged for assessing attitudes. Here are some of the major topics the authors used to group the various scales: "Social Practices" grouped scales measuring family-related practices, educational practices, and practices in economics. "International Issues" grouped measures such as political relations and international conflicts. The group "Political and Religious Attitudes" included scales for measuring attitudes toward specific ethnic and national groups. The category of "Significant Others" contained such topics as family, self and others, and status. The "Social Institutions" group discussed measures of legal institutions, health-related institutions, and religious and economic institutions. These topics represent only some of the groups discussed; many more attitude and opinion scales have been developed since this early compilation, and now governments and private-survey companies are assessing attitudes at the national and international levels. The amazing success of predicting voting patterns is testament to the high level of sophistication that attitude and opinion measurement has now attained.

There are several properties of the Thurstone–Chave technique that need to be highlighted because they will be important in the following sections of this book:

(1) ¯Participants can use ordered scales such as numbers, letters of the alphabet, or even verbal descriptions when they make judgments about statements of opinion.

(2) Assessing the frequency or proportion of categorical judgments works as well for verbal statements as it does for physical stimuli such as brass weights or a photograph of a woman.

(3) People's judgments of attitude statements, as seen on a Thurstone–Chave scale, fall directly in line with their behavioral commitments, such as church membership. These are key findings. They tell us a great deal about how our judgments are tied to our commitments, and they show us how seemingly simple judgment processes really are highly sensitive to the important parts of our life, especially those involving our emotions.

Note that Thurstone and Chave simply asked people about their church attendance and then used that simple rating to find out if there were differences in the patterns of attitude judgments made by frequent attendees and non-frequent attendees. There was no attempt to study hot-button, emotional topics, and certainly no attempt to analyze the judgment processes of highly biased partisans and extremists. But the techniques they pioneered in fact opened up ways for us to understand the judgment processes people experience when they have some sort of enduring connection and commitment to an issue.

The next chapter describes the thinking processes of radical hearers dealing with considerably more divisive issues.

CHAPTER 5

WHEN ATTITUDES AND THE SELF GET INVOLVED

T he Thurstone–Chave study of church attendees was truly a breakthrough in several ways: it showed that sophisticated questions about personal beliefs could actually be studied and that the responses of the participants could be analyzed with rigorous statistical methodology. For the first time, we could obtain a *quantitative* picture of what are in fact very personal and potentially very touchy beliefs. Matters of faith are among our deepest emotional issues, and the Thurstone–Chave approach showed that truly deeply held values could be opened up for more revealing experimental testing. This was a critical first step to gaining a good understanding of radical hearing.

In this chapter, I will discuss research that shows important differences between the mind of the "true believer" and the thinking and judging processes of people who are more moderate in their beliefs. There is a great difference between the two, as we shall see. I'll make the point, with data, that it is not *what* you believe but *how extremely you believe it* that is the key difference between highly involved partisans and people who are more moderate in their beliefs. While political commentators and the major political parties spend a lot of time and money to prove how different they are from their opponents (and how much better, of course), the research on radical hearing as it is presented in this book shows that they are in fact cognitively and emotionally nearly identical to each other. It is the moderates who are different from both. Data have shown that highly "pro" people are cognitively much more similar to highly "anti" people (and vice versa) than they are to moderate and uncommitted people.

The research required to uncover such an unusual conclusion

is difficult and sensitive. On emotional topics such as religion and politics, research methodology has to be carefully adapted to the sensitivities of investigating people's attitudes of deep personal significance. One frequently hears about science that should follow the gold standard of "random assignment" of research participants to experimental conditions so that there are no hidden biases that might distort the results of the experimenter's conditions. But that sort of consideration is completely at odds with the nature of the type of research questions involved in studying emotional biases. In fact, conducting judgment research of this sort is very difficult because it definitely does *not* employ random assignment. Instead, it requires the "known-groups" method. In other words, rather than trying to *avoid* having a biased sample in your study and employing a "random assignment" of participants to the various conditions, it is *precisely* biased samples that you want to recruit for your research on emotions. To study the effects of personal biases on judgment, you have to make sure that you actually recruit into your study *truly biased people.* You have to go into the community and find people who, by their behaviors and lifestyles, will proclaim to the world that they are "believers," that they will take and defend a personally emotional stand on the particular topic you plan to study. I will repeatedly mention the known-groups method in the upcoming chapters; in fact, in chapter 8, I will show how initially uncommitted boys, deliberately selected for not having any preexisting biases, in fact became radical and hostile "true believers" right in front of experimenters' eyes. Social conditions can create biased "known groups" as another way of studying radical-hearing processes. Since intergroup war erupted during the study of the boys, that method has proven its worth repeatedly.

If frequency of church attendance is an indicator of emotional commitment, the next logical step is to study the extent to which emotional commitments can bias judgments about statements when participants are directly asked about their feelings on the issue. Can a person with a known commitment, someone who we know is emotional about a particular issue, respond in a rational, cool, unbiased manner when he is making seemingly objective judgments about the issue? Furthermore, what kinds of judgment processes can we expect to see from someone who is strongly committed on one side of an issue compared to someone who has an opposite feeling about that issue? How might each of these people compare to someone who has no particular opinion on the topic? This question allows us to investigate "pro" and "con" attitudes, on one hand, and then to compare both of those attitudes against someone who has no particular opinion. The answer to this question is the single most important key to the nature of radical hearing.

One more point. Since small brass weights are not being judged, we would not call this type of experimental research a psychophysics study. It would be a *psychosocial* judgment study, since the emotional commitments to be investigated are statements about beliefs and values. I will use the term psychosocial throughout the remainder of this book. That language provides a framework for discussing a number of studies that demonstrate how emotions do in fact bias what would otherwise simply be rational thinking.

CIVIL RIGHTS, "PRO" AND "ANTI" STANDS, AND PSYCHOSOCIAL JUDGMENT PROCESSE

The foundational research study for addressing judgment processes involving partisan, emotionally committed people was conducted by Carl Hovland and Muzafer Sherif.[1] Their intent was to study the judgment processes of really involved, hot-under-the-collar activist partisans regarding the issue of racism. It is noteworthy that they conducted this study at the University of Oklahoma in the early 1950s. For one thing, Oklahoma is a border state that had a strong tradition of resistance to what is considered "federal interference," and racial issues at the time played into that resistance. Even more compelling, two landmark Supreme Court decisions had just come down concerning racial discrimination at the university's Law School. In the 1948 *McLaurin v. Oklahoma Board of Regents* case and the 1950 *Sipuel v. Oklahoma Board of Regents* case, attorneys for both McLaurin and Sipuel (Sipuel was represented by Thurgood Marshall, chief counsel of the National Association for the Advancement of Colored People) argued that neither man could get a legal education because the Law School excluded people of color. The more well-known 1954 *Brown v. Board of Education* decision followed the precedent of these two Oklahoma cases.

So when Hovland and Sherif undertook the project there was a lot of concern about "Negro rights" and "federal intervention" in that charged, emotional atmosphere. Fortunately for research purposes, there were highly emotional partisans on both sides of the issue who could be recruited for participation in the study. Interestingly, newspaper reports of the time suggest that the general college student body was not in an uproar over the issue of racism. That is an important point, because the atmosphere gave the experimenters a chance to also study the judgmental processes of neutral, middle-of-the-road people. This is the proper control group when the effects of extremely "pro" and extremely "con" attitudes are being compared, because it allows for a condition of noninvolvement and therefore representation of the middle-range of the judgment scale.

Hovland and Sherif were able to study the judgment processes of highly involved problack college students and some activist white students who had been supporting civil rights for blacks. (The authors used the terms "anti-Negro" and "pro-Negro" in their study; here, I use "antiblack" and "problack" to describe the groups that were against rights for black people and for rights for black people, respectively.) Some highly "antiblack" students were available from a local fraternity known for its exclusionist policies. Finally, a group of moderate white students who had not engaged in any kind of social activism volunteered to participate; they were scored as neutral or moderate on the issue, and they provided valuable data for comparison against the results from the partisans. With no particularly strong emotional involvement on the issue, they were not expected to show any noticeable pattern of judgmental biases.

Hovland and Sherif obtained a set of 114 statements expressing beliefs about the social position of blacks that had been employed in a study in Southern states in the 1930s, a period of American history known for its racist attitudes. The statements were deliberately chosen to range from extremely hostile and angry feelings about blacks, to neutral, middle-of-the-road feelings, to highly favorable and positive statements about blacks. The statements were typed onto 3 × 5 cards and put into a deck for easy handling by the participants. The researchers then gave detailed instructions on how the participants were to make judgments about the beliefs expressed in the statements. Below is an excerpt that should give you a good feel for how a psychosocial judgment study using real beliefs rather than brass weights is conducted:

> You are given a number of statements expressing opinions in regard to the social position of Negroes. These cards are to be sorted into different piles . . . with roman numerals on them. . . . Under Card 1 put those statements which are most unfavorable in regard to the social position of Negroes. . . . Under Card XI, put those statements which are most favorable. Use your judgment as to where each statement should be placed in the 11 piles.[2]

The results are displayed in figure 5.1, below.

The sorting of four groups are displayed in this figure, each labeled by group. As you can see from the top two graphs, there is an extreme judgmental bias. Even though there were 114 statements to be judged into the scale categories covering the full range of positions on the eleven-category scale, note how some participants grossly underused some of the judgment categories. If none of the judges had any biases, there would be about ten statements in each of the eleven categories, making for a pretty flat distribution. The actual results are very different from that, and are different in ways that are quite revealing of judgmental bias effects.

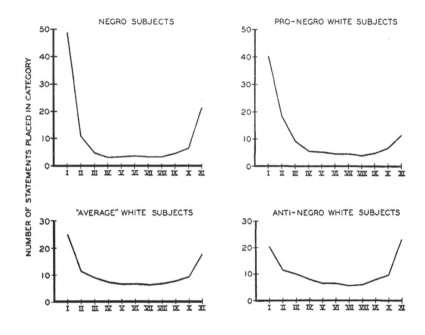

Figure 5.1. Number of statements assigned to each judgment category on the issue of the social position of blacks.[3]

The two groups of problack judges placed an average of forty to fifty statements in the antiblack end of the scale. This amounts to 40 to 50 percent of the entire set of statements going into one end-category. In the language of judgment research, those results display really poor discernment. The emotionally involved problack judges showed "lumping" of statements; but note that the lumping was at the end of the scale *opposite* to their own opinions. That group saw a large majority of the statements saying something opposite to their own opinions. Where did they get so many statements to create that lumping? They found them in the middle-range categories, the neutral, noncommittal statements, the statements that might have been made by moderates. You can see the very low frequencies of judgments in the middle range. Remember, these are *average* judgments from all the participants in that group. Some of the frequencies are as low as one, two, or three statements out of a total of 114 statements. These biased judges simply ignored or never even processed the middle categories. This is a vivid demonstration of how emotions warp what we hear (and judge). The moderate, uncommitted judges did not demonstrate such biased patterns of judgments; they made more middle-category judgments, indicating that they could understand the meaning of moderate statements as just that: moderate. They showed some elevation of judgments at the ends of the scales (the so-called end effect, a standard finding in judgment studies), but they were much more able to see things as moderate than either of the more ego-involved sets of judges.

The meaning of these results is eye-opening and very relevant to what we are learning about radical hearing. If you deliberately study the most attitudinally involved people, as opposed to a random assignment of participants, then you will find that there is ignoring or under-using of middle-range, moderate categories of judgment. Equally significant are the results of the lumping at the "favorable" end of the sale. This is the judgment category that most nearly represents the opinions of the problack judges. This "own-end" of the scale contains relatively few statements judged as belonging in it; there are more than are in the ignored middle categories but certainly fewer than in the opposite-to-one's-own end of the scale. This suggests that there are relatively few statements of belief that we judge as acceptable to our own beliefs. Since the investigators made sure that there was a sufficient number of statements covering all categories, we would expect at least some reasonable number of them to be very favorable "to the social position of Negroes." While a few groups judged that way, it is obvious that that number of judgments is dramatically lower than the judgments that are considered opposite to one's own highly involving personal end of the scale. These groups simply *failed to* "discern and compare" those middle-of-the-range points of view. This is a way of showing how radical hearing functions. These highly partisan participants did not "hear" the statements at all in any meaningful way; they read them just enough to contrast them into the opposite end of the scale. I will rephrase that: they contrasted them into the *opponents'* end of the scale.

These data clearly show in graphic form what we know about radical hearers: "If you are not for me, you are against me." Literally. Having a reference scale biased by extremist emotions, it takes a radical or extreme statement of belief before a person can judge it as acceptable to his or her own point of view. Most beliefs are unacceptable to an extremist. To get such a person to accept someone else's point of view, that other person has to hold beliefs nearly as extreme, or more so, than the emotionally-involved believer. Anything else is heresy. In fact, the other person does not have to state an opinion or do anything to get rejected; just being insufficiently extreme is justification in the mind of the radical hearer for being cast into the nether region of the opposite end of the continuum of beliefs.

THE PROBLEM WITH "IMPOSED" CATEGORICAL JUDGMENT

In a second experiment, Sherif and Hovland reasoned that there was something quite significant about their first set of psychosocial judgment effects.[4] Although the more extreme participants may have appeared to be careless or inattentive in their judgments because of their lumping of statements, the investigators noted that the bias in judgments was occurring in the middle, the more ambiguous and unstructured part of the judgment scale. In fact, it appeared that use of a required, or forced, set of eleven distinctions was more likely a methodological problem, not a judgment problem. It seemed to them that the Thurstone–Chave technique of providing eleven categories for judgment, while perhaps sound from a psychometric approach, may not have been appropriate or the most revealing way for the committed participants to do their "discerning" and "comparing" as they made their judgments. The imposed external judgment scale could be forcing people to make distinctions that simply were not relevant to their way of viewing the world.

To respond to this possibility, Sherif and Hovland conducted a second study on the same issue and with the more committed types of participants, but this time they employed an unstructured, more open-ended technique for judging the statements. Accompanying the same deck of statement cards as was used in the previous study, they developed the following set of instructions explaining to the participants how they were to make their judgments:

> You are to sort the cards into the number of piles that may seem necessary to you so that the stand expressed on the issue of the social position of Negroes will be different from the other pile or piles. You may sort into any number of piles which in your judgment is necessary so that each pile of cards represents a different stand on the issue. Put statements into the same pile which belong together in terms of their relative stand on the issue, that is, favorable, unfavorable, etc. This should determine how many piles you have when you finish sorting.
>
> This means that when you are through sorting, you will have different piles of statements arranged in order from low or lowest to high or highest.[5]

There is something particularly impressive about this set of instructions. Note that there is no suggestion as to how many categories (distinctions) the participants were to make; decisions were to be made entirely at their own discretion. Again, I remind you of the topics about structure, order, and certainty presented in chapter 2. People need to have structure, meaningful order, and clearly defined patterns in their perceptions. But when you do not give them judgment categories to use for sorting through, for example, 114 statements, they rely on their own natural ways of seeing the world, and their minds will find a way to do it.

This is the "own-categories" technique, in which participants have to mentally provide their own categories for judgment and, in doing so, of course, they reveal the true nature of the distinctions, the discernment, and the comparisons they make. This provides perhaps the clearest, purest way of finding out how they think about their world; in this case, what they think about black people, about civil rights, about government policies for civic relations, and so on. The number of categories people use to make their judgments, and the patterns of the ways they use those categories, directly reflects their radical-hearing and judgmental processes.

As you might expect from the judgments of extreme partisans on this issue, the data showed significant intergroup differences in both the number of categories the participants created to make their judgments and the ways they used those categories. The more committed problack participants used, on average, four categories or fewer, whereas the less-committed white participants used five or more, a statistically significant difference. The committed judges had a simpler category system to discern differences and comparisons among the statements of opinion. Even more revealing was the *actual frequency of use* of the categories: how frequently each category was used to judge the "pro," "neutral," and "anti" beliefs expressed in the statements. The results of this study are displayed below in figure 5.2.

To analyze the results, investigators plotted the number of times each category was used for the two types of participants among the problack and moderate participants: those who used very few categories and who showed the poorest discriminations—a judgment version of "simple-mindedness" (three categories), and those who used a larger number of categories (six), people who apparently were more "open-minded" in their judgments of the meaning of the statements. But you may be surprised to see how what appears to be a more open-minded performance of the biased people actually turns out to be perhaps not so open-minded. We have to look carefully at how the statements were judged, and we see that bias can be bias even when it does not initially look that way.

The graphs in figure 5.2 are actual visual representations of the "discerning and comparing" concepts discussed earlier; they show "judgment in action." To interpret the figures: the category labeled "I" represents the "antiblack" end of the scale, and category "III" is the problack end. Two aspects of judgment show up simultaneously in these pictures: we can compare highly committed versus neutral judges, and we can see how many judgment categories were actually needed by these two groups to "discern" and "compare" attitude-relevant statements.

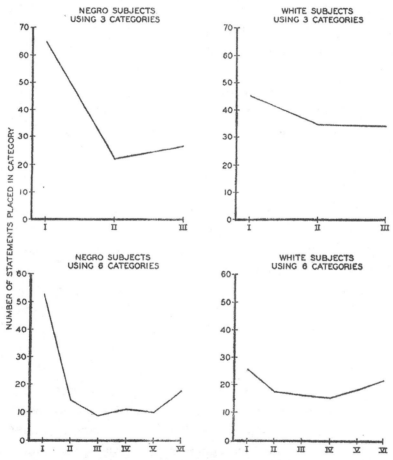

FIG. I. DISTRIBUTIONS OF NUMBERS OF STATEMENTS ASSIGNED TO EACH CATEGORY BY NEGRO AND WHITE JUDGES WHO CHOSE EITHER THREE OR SIX AS THE NUMBER OF CATEGORIES NEEDED TO REPRESENT DIFFERENCES AMONG STATEMENTS CONCERNING SOCIAL POSITION OF NEGROES

Figure 5.2. Frequencies of placement of statements of opinion about the social position of blacks, employing the "own-categories" technique. Data are plotted for groups using three categories and six categories.[6]

The top two graphs display the results from the judges of both samples of participants who used a constricted judgment scale of only three categories. Even though some participants showed "poor discernment" by needing only three categories to judge the large set of 114 attitude statements; nevertheless, those who were more moderate on the issue—the neutral white judges—did not show any particular lumping of statements. Even though they needed only three categories to make their judgments, they were more even-handed in making those judgments to distinguish among the various stances on the issue.

But the highly involved problack judges showed a very strong bias; they placed about sixty-five statements (a huge 57 percent into *one* single category, and, of course, that category was at the end opposite of their own opinions). This is a glaring example of the contrast effect. And obviously the lumping occurred because the judges virtually ignored the middle-range statements, category II. There just were not that many neutral statements in the set, according to them; they could not "see" them as neutral, and so they judged them as being at the opposite end of the scale, thus, the contrast effect.

The results of the participants in the six-category judgment are presented in the bottom two graphs. Again, the category labeled "I" is the "anti" end of the scale, and category "VI" is the "pro" end of the scale. For the neutral white participants, there is no distinct pattern of bunching of statements; the six categories are fairly evenly used. This is judgmental "even-handedness." But a pattern of bias, lumping, is shown in the distributions of the problack judges. Even though they used double the number of categories—six—as the three-category problack participants did, there is nevertheless a clear pattern of lumping, again at the end of the scale opposite their own personal attitudes. Apparently, their "open-mindedness" that led them to use more categories for their judgments nevertheless showed significant biasing effects. Here is the contrast effect again. Perhaps nowhere else in the social-science literature has the true nature of black-and-white thinking been so clearly demonstrated. (I intend no pun with that comment.)

These simple categorizations and high instances of bunching-up of opposing statements show the dangers of radical hearing, the loss of consideration for moderate points of view. After all, why should a person think very deeply and make fine-grained distinctions among points of view when that person regards those opinions as opposed to his own? Since these statements have been contrasted away to the evil opponents' end of the scale, they can be ignored or suppressed, and certainly not given any credibility; they cannot have any influence on a radical hearer's judgment.

THE CONCEPT OF "THRESHOLD"

The psychosocial judgment model gives us one more technical distinction that we can make about detecting judgmental bias. In traditional judgment literature, the concept of *category threshold* describes the relationship between the intensity of the stimulus and the sensitivity of the judgment category itself. You have heard of "subliminal stimulation," the notion that some stimuli may be too subtle or weak for us to consciously detect but that may still have a sensory influence on us. A five-gram weight may be too small to call "medium," but it could be judged as "light." How much heavier would it have to be to be called "medium"? Six grams, eight grams, eleven grams? The point of actual weight it takes to move into the heavier category is a measure of threshold sensitivity. In the Tresselt study (chapter 3), the jewelers had a lower threshold of sensitivity for their judgments of "medium," but the weightlifters had a higher threshold.

A similar model translates directly into psychosocial judgment, as Sherif and Hovland demonstrate with their results. For the most partisan, emotionally involved problack judges, we can say that their threshold of very favorable "to the social position of Negroes" was very much *raised*; they saw only a very few statements of belief as being strong enough to be considered "favorable." On the other hand, their threshold of judging "anti" statements was very low; it was easy for them to judge opinions different from theirs as being "opposite" of them and therefore easily lumped into the "anti" category. Moderate judges do not carry around with them particularly high or low thresholds, and so they do not experience the perceptual biases that more involved judges do. In this model of radical hearing, then, the effect of ego involvement leads to raised thresholds of judging beliefs as similar to one's own, and to lowered thresholds for judging things as opposite to one's own stance. These concepts will be useful shortly, when I discuss studies in which people are asked point-blank to indicate what they find personally acceptable and what they choose to reject.

WHERE DOES THE BIAS COME FROM?

The judgment model and the two studies by Sherif and Hovland fit the psychosocial model perfectly, using psychophysical techniques for judging social beliefs. But there is one question here. Let me refer to a point I made earlier. All judgment is not absolute; it is comparative. So what is the comparison standard in this type of study? What is causing the reference scale to become so distorted and biased? Recall the Tresselt study: strong, muscular weightlifters required a heavier brass weight to be judged as "medium" than did jewelers. The backgrounds of the two groups had set different standards for calling something "medium." In the social-attitudes judgment study, the reference scale was set not by physical strength but by mental strength coming from the emotional intensity of radical thoughts and beliefs.

The data of these studies show that the participants' reference scales are biased in making category judgments, and something has to be infused into those reference scales to cause that biasing. How does this work? The logic of the model leads to the conclusion that it has to be the person's own opinion, her attitude and, by extension, her deeply held value, her very self-concept that is operating as an *internal anchor*. Our concept of who we are, of what we value the most anchors our lives, our goals, our motivations, and our judgments; the Thurstone–Chave category judgment technique shows vividly how our beliefs anchor, literally, our judgments. That is why I devoted some discussion to the endorsement process in chapter 1. It is important to reiterate the point made in the earlier discussion of the Thurstone–Chave technique. At no point did those experimenters or Sherif and Hovland directly ask the participants to use their own attitudes as anchors. Personal opinions were never suggested as comparison stimuli. So here we find the key to the sorts of biases we have been seeing in these studies. The answer lies in the person's own attitudes and emotional commitments; it is the person's beliefs, unbidden by the experimenters, that lodge in the judgmental system that defines his or her personal reference scale and become the anchor point on that scale. All else is judged against that point, and experimental instructions are not required to make that linkage occur.

In the unstructured world of making judgments about statements of opinion, one's own opinion stands out as the point of comparison, even if the person is not aware of it. Thurstone himself argued that personal opinions and beliefs should be kept out of the judgment process because they might bias it. Exactly! That is precisely the point Sherif and Hovland wanted to make; bias is inevitably going to be there if you are dealing with what I call radical hearers. By deliberately *not* making personal opinions part of the equation, the techniques provide a clear and compelling picture of how subtly yet effectively *attitudinal bias* operates in the hearing and endorsing process.

Our concept of who we are, of what we value the most—our self-concept and its connected emotional involvement—anchors our lives, our goals, our motivations, and our judgments. Assimilation and contrast effects revolve around our own personal anchorage—that ego-involving stance that organizes our perception of the world.

Since our anchors warp and bias our judgment scale when they are extreme, it would be more accurate to say that they organize our *mis*-perception of the world. Moderate, nonpartisan judges have no strong, biasing emotions in their judgment scales.

THE CONCEPTS OF "LATITUDE OF ACCEPTANCE," "LATITUDE OF REJECTION," AND "LATITUDE OF NONCOMMITMENT"

There is yet another interesting aspect of these findings. A positive feature of this "own-categories" kind of research requires us to rethink what we mean by the concept of "attitude." One of the major shortcomings of common-sense thinking about people's attitudes is to assume that they "have an attitude," and that implies that what they believe can be represented by a statement of liking or disliking something, a check mark on a scale, or a simple response of "Yes" or "No" to a survey's question about whether or not they "have an opinion" about a particular topic. But from a judgment perspective, attitude assessment is not simply an isolated, single-response affair. This model requires that we give the person a chance to indicate his acceptance (endorsement) of a *range* of opinion statements *along with* a range of rejections of statements that he does not accept *along with* a range of statements of opinion about which he may choose to ignore entirely. This insightful switch of approach requires an entirely different and much richer way of thinking about judgment and emotional bias.

THE ELECTION STUDIES

Allowing participants to use their own personal category system for revealing how they perceive the world provided a flexible technique. It guided researchers in a number of follow-up investigations on hot-button political issues, which were begun after the original studies on problack opinions. We can view those issues in the judgment framework provided by psychosocial techniques. Politics and religion are probably the hottest of hot-button topics in American society. The topic of politics cycles around every two and four years when there are elections. That is when attitudes and opinions boil up, certainly for the ego-involved partisans, as we saw in the study on the civil rights turmoil. That study gave Sherif and his colleagues a natural setting for testing their broader model of how attitudes influence judgments.

As with most elections, the 1956 national election in Oklahoma brought out emotionally charged political speech on the issues of the day. Knowing ahead of time that emotions would get hot on both the Democratic and Republican sides of the issues, the investigators developed a set of statements covering the full range of opinions, from "extremely favorable to Republicans" to "middle-of-the-road" to "extremely favorable to Democrats."[7]

First, here are the statements themselves:

A. The election of the Republican presidential and vice-presidential candidates in November is absolutely essential from all angles in the country's interests.

B. On the whole, the interests of the country will be served best by the election of the Republican candidates for president and vice-president in the coming election.

C. It seems that the country's interest would be better served if the presidential and vice-presidential candidates of the Republican party are elected this November.

D. Although it is hard to decide, it is probable that the country's interests may be better served if the Republican presidential and vice-presidential candidates are elected in November.

E. From the point of view of the country's interests, it is hard to decide whether it is preferable to vote for presidential and vice-presidential candidates of the Republican party or the Democratic party in November.

F. Although it is hard to decide, it is probable that the country's interests may be better served if the Democratic presidential and vice-presidential candidates are elected in November.

G It seems that the country's interests would be better served if the presidential and vice-presidential candidates of the Democratic party are elected in November.

H On the whole the interests of the country will be served best if the presidential and vice-presidential candidates of the Democratic party are elected this November.

I. The election of the Democratic presidential and vice-presidential candidates in November is absolutely essential from all angles in the country's interests.[8]

The investigators recruited participants in the state of Oklahoma who were known to be highly partisan on election issues: two groups, the Young Republicans and the League of Young Democrats, plus a sample of moderates who were not taking partisan stands on the issues. The instructions required the participants judging the statements to make four types of endorsements. These were:

- to underline the one statement that comes *closest to their own stand;*
- to mark any other statements that are *acceptable* to them;
- to cross out the one statement that is *most objectionable* to them; and
- to mark any other statements which they find *objectionable.*[9]

Note that these instructions make *no* suggestion that all the statements had to be marked. The investigators took into consideration that there might be some stands about which a participant would choose to be noncommittal, and that was subtly expressed in the way the instructions are worded. So now we have systematic research directly asking the participants to express their opinions and to use them in making their decisions about the various stances on a hot-button issue. The innovation of this study was that participants had to make their own self-conscious attitudes a part of how they judged opinion-related statements. It turns out that this is a very revealing part of the effects of radical hearing.

The simple methodological innovation of asking participants to consider attitude-relevant statements in this threefold judgment procedure results in three very different views of endorsement and three different ways of finding out how attitudes influence judgment. Here are the ways these endorsement components were defined by the investigators:

> Latitude of acceptance is the position on an issue (or toward an object) that is most acceptable, plus other acceptable positions.

> Latitude of rejection is the most objectionable position on the same issue, plus other objectionable positions.

> Latitude of noncommitment, defined as those positions not categorized as either acceptable or objectionable in some degree.[10]

The results of this new way of analyzing judgment processes are displayed in figure 5.3, below.

The height of the bars indicates the average number of statements within each latitude, demonstrating how inclusive each latitude is for any particular group of participants. The results are displayed for participants who endorsed as their most acceptable position either "A" or "B" (extremely pro-Republican), those who endorsed the middle-of-the-range positions ("D," "E," and "F"), and those extremely pro-Democrat participants who endorsed positions "H" or "I." Note that there are three sets of bars in each graph. The leftmost graph displays the results for the endorsements for the *latitude of acceptance*, the middle set shows the results for the statements the participants ignored and did not judge as either acceptable or objectionable (the *latitude of noncommitment*), and the rightmost graph shows the results for the *latitude of rejection*. Finally, note that the height of the bars—representing the average number of judgments—could go from 0 (no statements checked at all) to 9, since there were nine statements to be judged. If you think of these bars as proportions of the possible nine statements, you can see how low some proportions are compared to how high others are.

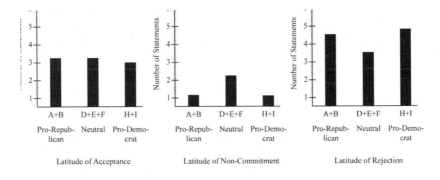

Figure 5.3. Average number of statements placed in their latitudes of "acceptance," "noncommitment," and "rejection" by participants who endorsed statements at the "extreme," "pro," and "neutral" positions in the 1956 national election.[11]

Now to interpret the results. First, concentrate on the extremist judges: the pro-Republicans (those who endorsed positions "A" and "B") and the pro-Democrats (those who endorsed "H" and "I"). These two groups of participants reveal the most about the effects of radical hearing on judgments. They should be compared against each other and against the neutral participants, those who endorsed positions "D," "E," and "F." In the graph on the far left, note that all three groups had about the same number of statements that they endorsed as acceptable: their latitudes of acceptance. What the graph cannot show is *which* statements these are; however, other analyses show that the pro-Republican judges are endorsing pro-Republican statements and the pro-Democrat judges are endorsing pro-Democrat statements to nearly the same degree. It turns out that each group found about three of the nine statements to be acceptable, but these are diametrically opposing statements. Just by looking at the frequency of responses, it is clear that the latitude of acceptance as a raw number does not reveal any particularly interesting difference between extreme and moderate groups of participants, nor between the two groups of the extreme partisans. The raw number of "I accept this" judgments does not differentiate the extremist groups. (Many other studies on other topics by other investigators show this same effect. I will not discuss them here because they are solidly supportive of the points I am making. The interested reader will find an excellent survey of many of these studies in Alice Eagly and Shelly Chaiken's comprehensive *The Psychology of Attitudes*.[12])

Next, the middle graph shows, again, that the extreme groups ("A" and "B" and "H" and "I") do not differ from each other at all. They are noncommittal regarding only about one statement of the nine! But the moderate participants have almost double the number of statements they do not endorse. These are dramatic results. They show that the extremist partisans *choose not to be noncommittal* when they are judging attitude-relevant statements; they make a commitment to nearly everything that is presented to them. Extremely partisan people are *not noncommittal* when their attitudes are involved; they judge nearly everything as either for them or against them, and neutral statements cannot escape their acceptance and rejection tendencies. We saw this same effect earlier: simple, two-category thinking with lumping up of statements into end-categories. Now we can see that the latitude of noncommitment is very small in biased partisan participants *at both ends of the scale.* But when noninvolved and more moderate people read exactly the same statements with exactly the same experimental instructions, more neutral and objective judges do not show such judgmental bias: for them, there genuinely *is* a middle ground.

Finally, in the rightmost graph, we see the results for the latitude of rejection. Again there is a strong similarity in judgment of the extremist participants who are virtually identical in the *high* number (and high proportion) of statements that they judge to be objectionable. Note how many more statements they reject compared to the smaller number they find acceptable and, of course, the number they do not judge at all. Now, the neutral judges (categories "D," "E," and "F") also have somewhat more statements that they reject than they feel neutral and noncommittal about, but the number they reject is just about the same number as in their latitude of acceptance—a bit more than three, in both cases. What this shows is that middle-of-the-road judges both accept and reject about the same number; they are much more "even-handed" in how they view the world of political statements, and they do not display any particular bias against each end of the scale. And as I just said, they tend to be less driven to make a judgment about each and every belief related to their own position on the issue than either group of the more extremist participants. Extremists and partisans are likely to have problems with such people. Some people dislike someone who "won't take a stand." American political parties involved in voting campaigns virtually require that their candidate be identified with the phrase "You know where he [or she] stands." "He" usually stands at the extreme end of the attitudinal spectrum—at least until "he" gets elected.

The language of thresholds that I discussed earlier in this chapter is particularly useful to use to think about when considering the concepts of latitudes. The effect of highly partisan beliefs is to raise one's threshold for her latitude of acceptance and to lower the threshold for her latitude of rejection. With the latter, for instance, it is very easy for a statement of belief to be contrasted away into one's latitude of rejection because the threshold for it is so low. Emotional hatreds and loves shift our thresholds, lowering them for things we dislike, and raising them so that we find relatively few things we can truly accept as our own. Our sensitivities in our judgment processes are based on where our thresholds get set, and those thresholds follow directly from the endorsement processes and commitments that we freely make and the values and commitments that are established as a result of our endorsements. I will discuss thresholds again in the next chapter, where I will look at research showing how partisan judges not only reject the beliefs of others; they also judge those beliefs as "unfair," "untrue," and "biased"; to the partisan mind of a radical hearer, the opponents really cannot get any grounds of credibility. No wonder the data are telling us that emotions warp what we hear.

IT IS NOT WHAT YOU BELIEVE BUT HOW MUCH YOU BELIEVE IT

With these data, we now have major insight into radical hearing and into the question I raised earlier in this chapter about just how different "opponents" on a hot-button issue are from each other and the comparison between them and moderates. The clearest message from the data of these studies and many others is that it is not "pro-Republican-ness" or "pro-Democrat-ness" that differentiates radical hearing and judging from less-biased hearing and judging; it is emotional involvement *itself* that sets up people for biased hearing. People who are partisans show biased radical hearing no matter which end of the attitude scale they endorse. Extremity is the dominant force in their hearing, and they are not different from each other in this respect. Both groups are different from more moderate and neutral people—the natural comparison group—who can show unbiased, fair, and balanced hearing. The main conclusion is that the key to radical hearing lies in the distinction between extremist partisans and moderates.

DO OTHER ISSUES GET THE SAME RESULTS?

We might want to be cautious in accepting the results of this single study. The results might not be able to be reproduced at another time or during another election, or they might just be specific to the people and the issues of the time and place. Fortunately, another golden opportunity for repeating the study occurred: the next national presidential national election, in 1960. This election was another windfall for Carolyn and Muzafer Sherif and their colleague Roger Nebergall[13] because their use of the known-groups method again fell right into line with the competitors in that election—maybe even more intensely than they would have with other elections. This time, the Democrats' nominee was John F. Kennedy, and the Republican nominee was Richard Nixon. So many emotional issues were involved in the events surrounding this election: Kennedy's Catholicism, Nixon's reputation as a "Red baiter," not to mention the fact that the end of the eight-year Eisenhower presidency had created great uncertainty about which way the country would go. All these emotional issues were wrapped up in the highly charged political atmosphere of the time, so when the investigators sought people with opposing attitudes, they had little trouble finding them.

The experimenters repeated the procedures of the study on the 1956 election, with similar sampling of partisans and moderates. Again, the investigators made sure that some of the participants were members of the League of Young Democrats or Young Republicans. They asked the participants to judge the statements with the number of categories they needed to distinguish the different opinions being stated among the various sentences. The data are displayed in figure 5.4.

Although four years had passed since the initial study, the results displayed in figure 5.4 show an amazingly close correspondence with the data of that earlier study. The latitude of acceptance data showed, again, little differences between the groups. The latitude of noncommitment data showed clear results: the moderate participants judged a significantly greater number of statements in the noncommittal category, while the extreme "pro" and extreme "con" groups underused this category significantly, and each group did so to the same degree. Finally, it is the latitude of rejection where we again see the sharply visible overuse of this category of judgment: both committed groups judge a high proportion of the overall nine statements as unacceptable to their own opinions, and both groups do so to the same degree—and, significantly, more than the neutral judges do. Overall, then, we again find that *underuse* of noncommittal judgments and *overuse* of unacceptable, rejecting judgments are highly characteristic of strongly committed radical hearing.

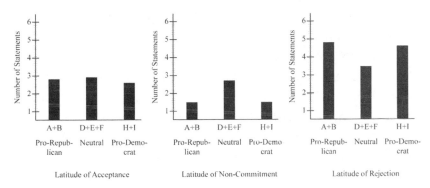

Figure 5.4. Average number of statements placed in their latitudes of "acceptance," "noncommitment," and "rejection" by participants who endorsed statements at the "extreme," "pro," and "neutral" positions in the 1960 national election.[14]

THE POWER OF THE LATITUDE OF NONCOMMITMENT

In chapter 2, I presented some basic ideas from the research on the psychology of personality concerning the need of some individuals to have structure and orderliness in their lives. Such a pattern of needs and motivations leads people with this style of living to be more concrete and well-structured in their beliefs and their perceptions of the world, as opposed to people who prefer to have uncertainty, lack of structure, and unpredictability in their lives. The judgment research shows clearly that emotional involvement can result in the same effects: simpler reference scales and a breakdown of fine-grained distinctions when judging attitude-related statements of belief.

One could interpret the results of the latitude of noncommitment as being very supportive of these findings. The data basically says that highly involved people avoid the ambiguity and lack of structure of not responding to some of the statements (those in the middle, of course), so they make a definite "accept" or "reject" judgment of nearly all the statements. In other words, nothing "gets by" them: they display a strong need to judge nearly everything, one way or the other. On the other hand, people who are more moderate, less committed, and therefore less emotional about the topic are apparently comfortable *not judging*; they can let the world go by without feeling compelled to judge it. Voices of moderation have a greater chance of being heard by people who have an open-minded approach toward deciding what the various opinions are on an issue. These are people who do not automatically reject ideas by contrasting away others' beliefs and values, which they themselves may not particularly endorse as being within their own personal latitude of acceptance. Conversing with ego-involved "judgmental people" is sometimes difficult: you just can't seem to find a topic that does not stir up a heated response from them. One of the most interesting results from these studies on the latitude of noncommitment is that we have a new but subtle angle on seeing how radical hearing operates. Of course, the latitude of rejection is the most glaring effect of radical hearing: highly committed people reject as unacceptable most of what they hear. But there is a group of other kinds of judgments they make about statements of belief, and these other facets of the effects of involvement are equally revealing about how biases operate to cast out the opponents. I will present research on these other ways of studying bias in the next chapter.

CHAPTER 6
OTHER ISSUES, OTHER EFFECTS, STILL THE SAME PRINCIPLES

One of the hallmarks of trustworthy science is the search for reproducible results. If the results from one study are to be trusted, they have to be tested and proven in additional studies to repeat the same pattern found in the original study. The results I have presented here from three studies—the social position of blacks and the two national elections—certainly do show significant repeatability. Thus, the principles of judgmental bias we have derived from these studies seem highly conclusive. Ego-involved people tend to engage in black-and-white, two-category thinking, and they have a wide latitude of rejection while letting few opinions escape their evaluative, judgmental tendencies.

But times change, issues change, and people change. The insights we have from radical hearing will be even more convincing if they are tested in different domains of hot-button issues. In this chapter, I will discuss results from three studies that involved very different issues and very different samples of people: emotional partisans favoring or opposed to the sale of alcohol, prounion and antiunion partisans, and rural versus urban partisans on the issue of legislative reapportionment. Following that, I will describe studies on yet more ego-involved samples, but these studies will show that there is much more to radical hearing than reference-scale biasing effects. Other outcomes of emotional attitudes show that they also lead the partisan radical hearer to undercut and denigrate the motivations they perceive to be behind what their opponents believe. That is, studies show that highly ego-involved judges believe their opponents are making weak arguments for their "wrong" side, they think their opponents are biased and unfair, and they think their opponents are not even telling the truth. Given these data, it is no wonder that we cannot seem to get along with our opponents; when we are ego-involved, we reject the very intellectual grounds on which our opponents stand.

THE CONSEQUENCES OF PARTISAN "WET" AND "DRY" ATTITUDES

The first study came from the same Muzafer Sherif/University of Oklahoma research team, but the hot-button topic they investigated may strike the reader as somewhat quaint or dated: the morality of selling and drinking alcoholic beverages. To the people of Oklahoma, who were very much against this issue in the early 1950s, a voter proposition for the ballot to legalize the sale and use of alcohol represented a strong threat to their deep religious values (and, I would say, a threat to their ego-involvement). In fact, some areas of the United States are still legally "dry," and the sale of alcohol is forbidden; in other regions, alcohol is allowed but only under highly regulated conditions. Perhaps the perceived "quaintness" is in the eyes of beholders, where the issue never even arose. But this was a deeply serious issue to a lot of Oklahoma voters.

The issue of allowing the sale of alcohol to become legal was bitterly fought by religious conservatives and, of course, by the bootleggers who made small fortunes secretly bringing alcohol into the state—literally through backwoods roads. But the loss of tax revenue and the general disrespect for the law engendered by prohibition led some determined groups to oppose prohibition and to support legalization. This issue arose in Oklahoma roughly every three to five years for decades, and public votes on the issue repeatedly defeated any attempts to overturn the law and allow legal sales. As Will Rogers, nationally known humorist and Oklahoma native, stated, "The South is dry and will vote dry. That is, everybody that is sober enough to stagger to the polls will."[1]

For the vote on the issue, the foes of prohibition again geared up and conducted a serious campaign that looked like it might finally succeed in abolishing prohibition. This meant, of course, an intensely emotional campaign on both sides of the issue, lining up antigovernment, proreligion conservative groups against prorepeal, liberal residents and others such as law enforcement agencies that had been forced to spend much time, effort, and money on trying to catch the bootleggers and put them out of business.

To investigate social judgment processes in this maelstrom, Carl Hovland, O. J. Harvey, and Muzafer Sherif developed a balanced scale of nine statements covering the full range of opinions about alcohol:

A. Since alcohol is the curse of mankind, the sale and use of alcohol, including light beer, should be completely abolished.
B. Since alcohol is the main cause of corruption in public life, lawlessness, and immoral acts, its sale and use should be prohibited.
C. Since it is hard to stop at a reasonable moderation point in the use of alcohol, it is safer to discourage its use.
D. Alcohol should not be sold or used except as a remedy for snake bites, cramps, colds, fainting, and other aches and pains.
E. The arguments for and against the sale and use of alcohol are nearly equal.
F. The sale of alcohol should be so regulated that it is available in limited quantities for special occasions.
G. The sale and use of alcohol should be permitted with proper state controls, so that the revenue from taxation may be used for the betterment of schools, highways, and other state institutions.
H. Since prohibition is a major cause of corruption in public life, lawlessness, immoral acts, and juvenile delinquency, the sale and use of alcohol should be legalized.
I. It has become evident that man cannot get along without alcohol; therefore there should be no restriction whatsoever on its sale and use.[2]

As the "dry" (antialcohol) forces historically had been dominant in this issue, the investigators had little trouble in recruiting highly dedicated, ego-involved antialcohol participants. These included volunteers from the Woman's Christian Temperance Union, traditional foes of legalization. A group of Salvation Army members was also recruited, along with college-age students in strict denominational colleges and students undergoing training for the ministry. The "wet" (prorepeal) forces were selected from public colleges and some individuals known to the investigators to be in favor of repeal. (For readers who are curious, the "drys" won this particular election yet again, but soon thereafter a reformist governor exerted powerful influence in a later referendum, and the "wets" eventually won the battle.)

The researchers employed the Sherif–Hovland technique for measuring the judges' latitudes of acceptance, rejection, and non-commitment. All judgment studies to date had shown that the extreme partisan judges showed the identical but reflected opposite pattern of feelings about the beliefs being presented in the statements: a large latitude of rejection and a small latitude of noncommitment from the more extreme partisan judges. But this study was designed to answer a slightly different question than was investigated in the investigators' prior studies. The results in those studies were so consistent that they felt it was important to move to a more general approach to these biasing effects of high ego-involvement. They sought in this study to show that it does not matter if you have an extreme "pro" or an extreme "anti" stance; in other words, they wanted to determine if extreme partisans are more like each other, judgmentally, than they are like more moderate people. From a judgment perspective, it might be entirely justifiable to combine the two seemingly opposite groups into one sample of highly committed partisans, and then to compare the combined group against moderates. That is exactly what the data showed. The results are displayed in Figure 6.1.

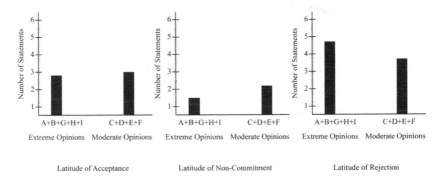

Figure 6.1. Average number of statements placed in their latitudes of "acceptance," "noncommitment," and "rejection" by the combined responses of participants with extreme opinions compared with participants whose opinions were more moderate.[3]

Note that there are only two groups of participants, "Extreme Opinions" (both the "wets" and the "drys") and "Moderate Opinions." In the figure, the combined ego-involved drys ("A" and "B") and the extreme wets ("G," "H," and "I") are compared to the moderates ("C," "D," "E," and "F").

The predicted pattern appears quite clearly. There were no differences at all in the latitudes of acceptance. But the extremists (the combined group of partisan "pros" and partisan "antis") had smaller latitudes of noncommitment and greater latitudes of rejection than did the moderates. The key conclusion from these results is that it is not so much what you believe but how extremely you believe it. The key to radical hearing is not so much that someone is "very pro" or "very con" regarding a particular issue; it is that they are an extremist, *per se*. Compared to moderate people, extremists display decreased discernment and comparison abilities, contrasting away from their self-anchor position the majority of middle-range opinions, and casting many of the issue statements into their latitude of rejection. The data show that "opposites" are not really opposite at all; in terms of the logic of judgment processes, both sides are cut from the same cloth.

RIGHT-TO-WORK LAWS AND OPPOSITION THERETO

Yet another hot-button issue provided experimenters with a chance to extend the range of topics that judgment models could assess. In the state of Washington, Alvar Elbing investigated the opinions and judgment processes about the issue of right-to-work laws.[4] At this time in the early 1960s, business groups were active in getting laws written so that union membership could not be a requirement of employment. Of course, union activists highly opposed such laws. To support right-to-work laws would be, basically, an antiunion vote. Even to this day, there are occasional pockets of antiunion sentiment, as was seen during a 2011 Wisconsin budgetary battle over union rights.

Following standard judgment research methods, Elbing broadly surveyed the public reports about the issue and developed a list of nine statements covering the full range of opinion statements. He then recruited students from University of Washington's College of Business who were expected to oppose the issue, plus other samplings of students not known to be involved with the issue. The response-scale statements varied from the prounion side to neutrality to the antiunion side.

A. In order to protect the workers' democratic rights, it is absolutely essential that "Right-to-Work" laws be defeated.

B. On the whole workers' democratic rights will be best protected by the defeat of "Right-to-Work" laws.

C. It seems that workers' democratic rights will be better protected by the defeat of "Right-to-Work" laws.

D. Although it is hard to decide, it is probable that the workers' democratic rights will be better protected if "Right-to-Work" laws are defeated.

E. From the point of view of the workers' democratic rights it is hard to decide whether it is preferable if "Right-to-Work" laws are passed or defeated.

F. Although it is hard to decide, it is probable that the workers' democratic rights will be better protected if "Right-to-Work" laws are passed.

G. It seems that workers' democratic rights will be better protected by the passage of "Right-to-Work" laws.

H. On the whole workers' democratic rights will be best protected by the passage of "Right-to-Work" laws.

I. In order to protect the workers' democratic rights, it is absolutely essential that "Right-to-Work" laws be passed.[5]

Again, participants provided endorsements about these statements, and sufficient participants were found to provide judgment data. The results are displayed below in figure 6.2. Elbing separated the two groups of extremists to compare them against each other and against the moderates.

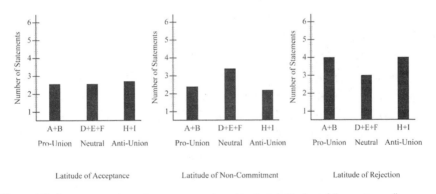

Figure 6.2. Average number of statements placed in their latitudes of "acceptance," "noncommitment," and "rejection" by participants who endorse statements at the "prounion," "neutral," and "antiunion" positions.[6]

Again we find the same pattern of results we have seen before: the latitude of acceptance was virtually the same for all groups, moderate judges had more middle-of-the-road statements within their latitude of noncommitment than the extremists did, and the extremist partisans placed more statements into their latitude of rejection than the moderates did. Both sets of extremists judged very few statements into their latitude of noncommitment. So, again, we see that the extreme partisans do not differ significantly from each other.

LEGISLATIVE REAPPORTIONMENT AND TAKING AWAY VOTES

In case you are not yet convinced of the validity of the judgment model, there is one final study on yet another issue that provides still more convincing evidence. During my graduate career with Muzafer Sherif and Carolyn Sherif, a hot-button political issue arose that provided us a natural environment for studying categorization effects. I obtained several measures in this study, the first of which I will discuss here. (I will report on the second measure, the speed of information processing, in the next chapter.)

At the time I completed my thesis in the early 1960s[7], the state of Oklahoma was under federal court order to reapportion its legislative districts. The state had experienced significant population growth after World War II, with the bulk of the population shifts concentrated in the major urban areas and the rural areas showing little growth. Yet the legislative districting for voting had not been changed accordingly, so the cities were left with much larger populations and reduced legislative representation.

The court order to correct that imbalance created a great deal of controversy, boiling down basically to a hot dispute between the cities versus the rural areas, which stood to lose power in the legislature should the court order be allowed to stand. During the heat of this battle, after extensive pretesting, I developed a standard set of sixty statements about the topic. I then went into the major urban areas and smaller communities in the rural areas to recruit pro-reapportionment participants and moderate participants to judge the statements by the own-categories procedure. To remind you, that technique instructs participants to use as many or as few categories as needed to judge the opinions in the statements. I assessed both the number of judgment categories that the participants used to make their judgments, and the sizes of their three latitudes.

Research like this has many complications, and I found that out the hard way. I conducted the study during a period of legal maneuvering by both "pro" and "anti" sides, and court decisions kept changing the dynamics of the conflict. A critical decision by a federal judge shifted the ground out from under the "anti" position. I will not go into the specifics of that decision, but the "anti" sides were forced to significantly alter their position of the issues. That may have been helpful to their side, but it rendered the data I had obtained from the "anti" side partisans useless because the change occurred as I was obtaining my data. Given that complication, I will report here only on the comparison of the "pro" partisans and the moderates. Life is sometimes hard for field researchers.

As you might expect by now, the results showed that the more involved participants tended to use fewer categories to judge than the uninvolved group: 74 percent of the proreapportionment group used four or fewer categories, whereas 76 percent of the uninvolved group used five or more categories. The results for the three latitudes are displayed below in figure 6.3.

As the graph shows, the latitude of acceptance was nearly the same size for both groups, but the latitudes of noncommitment for the uninvolved moderate participants were much greater than for the proreapportionment partisans, and their latitude of rejection was, again, much greater than that for the uninvolved moderates.

Although these patterns of data are no doubt familiar by now, they are of special interest because of one new aspect of the results. The "pro" forces were found to reside largely in activist civic groups such as the League of Women Voters in the urban areas. A questionnaire administered after the participants had completed their sortings showed that the proreapportionment group had an average education level of four years beyond high school and that the uncommitted moderates had an average level of five years. It is clear, then, that the participants in this study were in general quite highly educated, yet, interestingly, the same pattern of biases in judgment related to partisanship and ego-involvement occurred in their categorization processes. The evidence suggests, therefore, that the bias revealed by categorization techniques is relatively independent of one's level of education. Simple, two-category thinking appears even in highly educated but partisan people when they are emotionally involved. As Robert Zajonc noted (chapter 2), "affect is primary."[9]

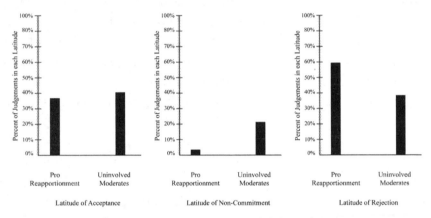

Figure 6.3. Average number of statements placed in their latitudes of "acceptance," "noncommitment," and "rejection" by participants who endorse statements at the "proreapportionment" and "uninvolved moderate" positions.[8]

SUMMARIZING ALL THESE STUDIES

Looking back over all the studies described in chapters 4 and 5, it is apparent that the effects of high partisanship and commitment are very consistent. These effects are among the most stable and repeatable anywhere in the social sciences. This consistency means that we have gotten a good handle on the fundamental judgment processes that are engaged when people become ego-involved on an issue. The reapportionment study also generated another type of data—level of education—and it also showed how emotions have a biasing effect on judgments independent of how much education the person has achieved. Bias is bias, no matter who has it.

WHY VOICES OF MODERATION CAN'T BE HEARD

The more unfortunate part of this "problems in communication" issue is that middle-ground statements, those in the realm of the moderate and the uncommitted, get lost in the biasing processes. As the graphs in the last few chapters have shown, the latitude of noncommitment is the smallest latitude. Moderate positions are not simply referred to as "moderate"; they are called "opposite to me" and are rejected as being opposed to one's own beliefs. This process is more or less locked in.

Why would someone listen to the voice of moderation when it is not seen as moderation? Moderation is seen as a belief that is opposed to a partisan judge's own side of the issue, and so it gets contrasted into the enemy camp and judged as opposing what one holds dear. Therefore, it is not even perceived as moderate. It is right there in the data plots in the figures. This is the essence of radical hearing.

But these latitudes are not the only way in which hearing is biased. What we have seen so far is the core finding about radical hearing, but there is more to it than the endorsement process. Not only does ego-involvement lead to biases and distortions in judging the "pro-ness" or "anti-ness" of statements, or their "acceptability" or their "objectionability"; there are many other ways in which the biases of partisanship show up in rejecting an opponent's speech and ignoring moderate speech.

OTHER FORMS OF RADICAL HEARERS' BIASES

The figures in chapter 5 neatly demonstrate that hot emotion "raises the bar" in changing the judgmental threshold of what an ego-involved person will accept and lowers judgmental thresholds for what they will reject. These effects show up clearly when radical hearers judge the beliefs (opinion statements) of neutral, middle-of-the-road speech; it is just not acceptable to them. The fact that highly ego-involved people have small latitudes of noncommitment reflects how emotion-based biases eliminate even the ability to perceive moderate beliefs. To ignore such beliefs simplifies judgments, eliminates ambiguities in judging, and reduces the complexity inherent in judging the beliefs of our opponents. This need for structure is pronounced when emotions are high. But ego-involvement biases are also deeply embedded in additional, and different, aspects of our thinking processes. In fact, when we judge someone else's beliefs, data show that if we are ego-involved, we cannot accept even the very grounds on which that other person stands. Why should you accept someone else's beliefs when you think they are biased and not telling the truth? Although the research I have presented so far shows that emotionally involved people have biased judgments, in this new research, it turns out that biased people think that it is other people who are biased! Of course, those "other people" are their opponents at the opposite end of the continuum of beliefs.

HOW FAIR AND UNBIASED ARE OUR FRIENDS AND OUR ENEMIES?

You will recall the issue of the "wets" versus the "drys" in the study of Oklahomans (by Hovland, Harvey, and Sherif).[10] The results for the latitudes of acceptance, noncommitment, and rejection were displayed in figure 6.1. The results of the prowet and prodry participants' latitudes mirrored almost exactly the pattern found in the studies about the two national elections, the right-to-work issue, and the legislative reapportionment issue.

Actually, this study was more elaborate and detailed and involved more than just asking the partisans on both sides to make acceptable/unacceptable endorsements of statements about alcohol. The investigators also wanted to investigate the actual thoughts that people had about the issue. To do this, they tape-recorded messages about the legalization of alcohol issue. These messages were put into the form of speeches presented by a person described as supporting a particular side of the issue. These fifteen-minute-long prepared talks about alcohol were carefully selected and pretested to make sure they represented the various "wet" and "dry" stances on the issue: one message was extremely in favor of legalization, one was extremely opposed to it, and one was middle-of-the-road.

The investigators wanted to discover the participants' opinions about the fairness and impartiality of these three sets of statements. These judgments assessed the extent to which the participants thought that the messages were (1) "reasonable or unreasonable," (2) "biased or unbiased," and (3) "propagandistic" or if they were "factual." These ratings were presented to the participants in order to assess their judgments after hearing each of the tape-recorded messages. The investigators then compared those ratings among the three groups of proalcohol, antialcohol, and moderate participants. The results of this study are displayed in figure 6.4 below.

The scale in each of the graphs represents the three types of messages the participants heard. The leftmost graph shows the most antialcohol position's message, the middle graph shows the moderate position, and the rightmost graph shows the most proalcohol message position. The three bars in each graph represent one of the groups of participants. The heights of the bars indicate the percentages of participants in that opinion group (proalcohol, moderate, or antialcohol) who rated the messages *as fair and unbiased*; the higher the bar, the more that they rated the message favorably by rating it as being fair and unbiased.

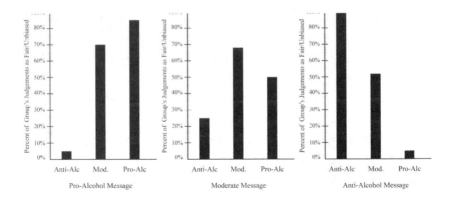

Figure 6.4. Ratings of how "fair" and "unbiased" messages about "antialcohol," "moderate," and "proalcohol" positions are as judged by proalcohol, moderate, and antialcohol participants.[11]

According to the authors: "It will be observed that there is an extremely close relationship between the individual's own stand on the issue and his evaluation of communication."[12]

Over 90 percent of the antialcohol participants group rated the antialcohol communication as fair and unbiased, but almost none of them rated the proalcohol communication that way. Similarly, and as you might expect, over 90 percent of the proalcohol participants rated the communication at the "pro" end of the continuum as fair and unbiased, and virtually none of them rated the antialcohol message as fair and unbiased. The moderate judges certainly rated down the antialcohol message, but a high proportion of them, roughly 80 percent, felt that the communication representing their own opinions was fair, with a slight down-rating of the extreme proalcohol message.

Interestingly, these data display that even moderates showed the same effect, rating highly as fair and unbiased the message that was near their own middle-range position. But their ratings of the extreme "anti" and extreme "pro" positions tended somewhat more toward fairness, showing that moderates do not appear to have such a strong drive to denigrate and disrespect viewpoints more extreme than their own. They are more balanced in their judgments of fairness and unbiasedness than the partisan proalcohol and antialcohol participants. So, for example, even if you do not have any particularly strong bias one way or the other; nevertheless, if someone is representing your own stand, mild as it is, you would tend to rate it as more fair and unbiased than you would rate the more extreme messages at the extreme ends of the attitude continuum.

In these data we again see the biasing effect of ego-involved attitudes, but these data show that biasing works on judgments of bias itself. It is easy to judge someone's opinions into your latitude of rejection if you think that they are saying something that is "unreasonable," that they were not being "factual" but "propagandistic" and "biased" in what they are saying. Note that these communications were not intended to directly attack a particular opponent's side of the issue. The taped talks were simply meant to provide a message about each side's stance, so there was no real reason to call the messages biased and unfair if they were just making a statement about the issue. But of course there was plenty of psychological reason. The reason was fused into the self-concepts and value judgments of the ego-involved judges. And, again, note the standard finding that we have seen in the previous studies: partisans on opposite sides of an issue behaved more like each other than they did someone who was more moderate. The graphs of the partisan judges are virtually mirror images of each other. It is ego-involvement and commitment, not the particular end of an opinion issue, where the extremizing effects of radical hearing are clearly revealed. After all, who can trust an opponent when that opponent is unfair and biased (at least in your opinion) in what they are saying?

MORE JUDGMENTS OF FAIRNESS: OTHER ISSUES

There are other ways to look at this phenomenon. A study on judgment of the truthfulness of statements about an involving issue was conducted by Carolyn Sherif and Norman Jackman.[13] Jackman, a sociologist, was skilled in observing the forces that being a member of a group can exert on individuals' thinking and judging processes. Jackman and Sherif wanted to find out if extreme attitudes (extreme versus moderate) would influence the type of judgments made about whether a particular statement was true or false. The qualities of "true" or "false" involve a different type of judgment than the qualities "fair and unbiased," but, regardless, there is the same tendency to downgrade and undercut an opponent's beliefs.

The topic of this study was also the legalization of the sale of alcohol, but the social conditions at the time were even more heated than those during the previous, similar study. An election on repealing the ban on alcohol sales in Oklahoma was in progress at the time this study was conducted, with all the publicity and public debate and hot emotions that those elections can stir up. The investigators recruited samples of both antialcohol, antirepeal participants and highly dedicated prorepeal participants (including members of a Christian temperance organization, church members who were antialcohol, and the "wets" who were prorepeal activists). So although the times and the populations had changed, the issue was still the same, and ego-involvement processes were at least at the same high pitch of intensity as before, perhaps even more so.

The investigators employed the same technique of having participants judge individual statements, but this time the judgment involved rating the truth or falsity of the statements. The study showed that both extreme "wet" and "dry" participants rated as false nearly 70 percent of the statements that were opposite their side. And, as predicted, they rated as true nearly 60 percent of the statements on their side. Wets rated as false 72 percent of the "dry" statements, and drys rated as false 74 percent of the "wet" statements. In fact, drys even rated as false 22 percent of the statements on their own side, and wets rated as false 22 percent of the statements on their own side! Apparently, both groups were showing very high standards for judging the truth of any statements at all about the issue, even rejecting some portion of them on their own side as less than "True." There is no doubt that they could not accept as true statements coming from the opposite side of the issue but it shows even more biasing effects of emotional involvement when your own "spokesperson" makes statements that you do not think are extreme enough to represent your own opinion. Extremists apparently need to make sure that their side is extremist enough or they will reject it as they reject their opponents' statements of beliefs.

ARGUMENT STRENGTH

Another way to think about bias effects is to get an estimate of how people perceive the strength of arguments made on both sides of an issue. This has been a concern in the arena of politics and social issues, where partisans need to know how the public is responding to their messages. Remember the discussion of the confirmation bias which I discussed in chapter 2. Charles Taber and Milton Lodge presented to their research participants a set of "pro" and "con" statements about the hot topics of affirmative action and gun control.[14] The participants also were asked to judge how strongly they thought that the statements were worded from "Very Strong" to "Very Weak." As you might predict, those participants who were supporters of a "pro" or "anti" stand on either issue rated the paragraphs on their own side of the issue as much stronger than they rated the strength of arguments on the opposite side of the issue. So we tend to regard our opponents' opinions as being weakly argued, and therefore not convincing.

RUSH TO JUDGMENT

The evidence for two-category, black-and-white thinking is compelling if for no other reason than that it is so consistent. Different investigators, different topics, different samples of participants at different times all converge to show the extent to which judgment ("discerning and comparing") is degraded into simple processing when people get ego-involved about an issue. Given all that, you might suspect that they would be "speed-readers" as well, quickly deciding what they like and do not like and rushing through the judgment task quickly. Emotions are primary, and they are quick to become aroused and then, in this case, shut down a person's judgment categories. That speed should show up in the categorization tasks used in social judgment research.

I tested this hypothesis as a second part of the study I conducted on legislative reapportionment in the state of Oklahoma. As you recall from my earlier discussion of that study, this was a particularly hot-button topic because rural areas of the state were going to lose some voting power; the recently exploding population in the state's larger cites was going to lead to a reapportionment of legislative seats if the initiative to change the election laws passed. Residents would be voting, in effect, to reduce the voting power of the rural districts, a genuinely upsetting thought among rural people; as one told me during my interview with her, "We take our politics seriously down here."

But this study had one angle that provided valuable new data. The attitude statements were typed on 3 × 5 cards for sorting into self-chosen categories they needed to judge the various statements of beliefs contained in the sentences (the "own-categories" technique). This made their "time on task" actually very visible so that I could easily see when they picked up the cards began their sorting and when they had sorted the last of their cards into their groupings. A handy stopwatch provided close timing of their judgment responses. Confirming the hypothesis, the more involved participants took an average of 14.8 minutes to complete their sorting, whereas the moderates took an average of 17.7 minutes, a difference of nearly 3 minutes. This is a 20 percent difference, with ego-involved judges reading and sorting (1) into fewer categories, thus showing poorer "discerning and comparing" and (2) faster processing, with less deliberation time expended. So it is not only black-and-white thinking, it is faster, quicker, black-and-white thinking. This is "rushing to judgment" and it happens when emotions are high. It is no wonder voices of moderation get lost in radical hearing; who wants to take the time to listen to someone we oppose who appears to be so biased, unfair, and saying untrue things?

BEHAVING IN LINE WITH YOUR COMMITMENT

With all these sorting and rating tasks, one might want to ask, "Where's the behavior?" to paraphrase a now-classic advertisement for hamburgers. What about trying some actual behavioral activity to see if partisans would actually go to the trouble to do something related to their attitude? Can extreme beliefs inspire or provoke people into making commitments to action? If a person is a true partisan, how likely are they to put their ego-involvement into action? This could be the ultimate source of where social action has its beginning.

Positioning the question this way raises the issue of "attitude-behavior consistency," a question of long-standing interest to research psychologists and marketing specialists. If you can influence someone's attitude, does that automatically mean that you can get their behavior to go along with it? There is a body of psychological research which shows that in fact the two realms are not always that closely related to each other (Alice Eagly and Shelly Chaiken have comprehensively summarized this research.[15]) But Carolyn Sherif and her colleagues thought that in fact these two components of belief would become more closely tied together if they engaged their research participants in issues of high ego-involvement.

To tackle this tough issue, Merrilea Kelly (cited in Carolyn Sherif et al.[16]) asked groups of female Pennsylvania State University students to pick out of a list of twenty current topics the ones that they felt "extremely interested or concerned about" and "extremely disinterested or unconcerned about." From one to three weeks after that rating session, each student was sent a letter informing her that an organizational meeting was going to be held on a particular topic, and asking if she would be interested in attending such a meeting. The results showed that 22 percent of the students actually attended the group meeting when the topic was one that they had earlier checked as interesting, but only 8 percent of the students attended the meeting where earlier they had rated to topic as uninteresting. This is about a 2.5 times increased actual behavioral response rate for topics the person rates as extremely interesting compared to topics felt not to be interesting.

College students are busy with many different alternative activities that pull them in different directions. It is not much of a surprise to learn that less than 10 percent of them would commit their time to go to a group discussion. But when they were highly interested in the topic, the number doubled. What you have here is a real-world example of behavioral commitment linked closely with ego-involvement and what the individual values. This may be one reason why you see so few Democrats at the Republican convention, or so few atheists at a Christian meeting, and so on.

CAN WE TRULY SEE THE OTHER PERSON'S POINT OF VIEW (OR, CAN WE WALK IN THEIR SHOES)?

There is an even deeper way in which radical hearing can harm interactions with others who have attitudes different from our own, especially when ego-involvement has flared up. How can we accept other people's points of view if we do not genuinely understand their beliefs? Would our communications with (different) others be more effective if we could see the world from their point of view and not from just our own?

So far, most of our examples have in one way or another involved judgment processes or endorsement processes that people make when they are presented with statements representing the opponent's position. That has made our approach to radical hearing a seemingly rather passive one: the participant judge is passively responding to speech about ego-involving topics. The Kelly study showing that people are motivated to actually do something about their beliefs does extend our understanding up by showing that our behavioral commitments follow our emotional commitments. But research has gone even deeper into the ways that we think about our opponents' beliefs. Can we genuinely understand our opponents? Can we think through and formulate the opponent's point of view? So the question is, does ego-involvement extend to biases in how the hearer actually construes their own version of the other sides' position?

This question of how an ego-involved person hears and construes an opponent's position operates at a pretty high level of mental abstractness. Do ego-involved people have distortions not only in what they hear but also in how they themselves would create the other side's positions? This is a question of how well can a person "walk in the other person's shoes," especially when that person dislikes if not actually hates that other person's point of view.

This is an important question because it helps reveal the depth of distortion and bias in the mind of the radical hearer. So in addition to asking ego-involved people to commit to going to a meeting on an involving topic, we also want to see if they can actually construct the point of view of their opponent. If they can do it, then it shows that the principles of biased hearing I have been discussing may be limited only to judgments of acceptance, rejection, and noncommitment and the judgments of fairness, strength, and truthfulness that I have just discussed. But if they cannot do it, if people basically cannot accurately grasp what their opponent is saying (over and above the tendencies to rate down the truth and bias underlying their statements of opinion and beliefs), then that shows that ego-involvement has even deeper cognitive effects, in fact actually damaging rational thinking about where the other person is "coming from."

This question was answered in a remarkably insightful study by Robin Dawes, David Singer, and Frank Lemons.[17] The study was conducted at a time when American society was nearly torn apart by the war in Vietnam. No topic has been more hot-button in recent memory. The American people had pretty much divided themselves into "Hawks," the prowar side of the issue, and "Doves," people very much opposed to the war who were calling for the government to withdraw from the war. Polarized feelings dominated daily communication, and the political ramifications reached all the way to the White House and the elections. In fact, to this day, the debate over American policy in Vietnam still stirs up hot emotions.

The first question addressed in this study was the issue of extremizing. Do advocates of these prowar and antiwar stances show contrast effects of each others' positions? As you know, contrast effects in judgments means that differences get exaggerated, and in the case of social judgments, one's own opinion acts as an anchor that makes other people's opinions different from it seem even more different. In their first study, Dawes, Singer, and Lemons studied how these polarized groups of prowar and antiwar students thought about how radical or extreme the various opinions on the issue were; it was a study about the perceived extremity of prowar and antiwar statements. To do this, in preliminary studies they developed sets of extreme, moderate, and mildly prowar and antiwar statements covering the full range of opinions on the war to be used in this study. Here are some examples from the larger complete set:

Extreme Hawk Statements:
1. Only fools and cowards can fail to see that we must defeat the Communists in Vietnam.
2. No American can in good conscience oppose our efforts in Vietnam; those who do are, in a word, cowards.

Moderate Hawk Statements:
1. Successful fulfillment of our commitment to Vietnam is necessary if other nations are to respect our national honor.
2. Peace can come to Vietnam only if United States military intervention is maintained.

Mild Hawk Statements:

1. Although mistakes are being made by the United States in Vietnam, we seem to be following a reasonable course there.
2. The advantages of our Vietnam policy somewhat outweigh its disadvantages.

Extreme Dove Statements:

1. United States intervention in Vietnam is ethically immoral, internationally illegal, and in violation of our own constitution. We should get out now.
2. We should get out of Vietnam now, without concern for "face" or prestige, or any other of those nonsensical abstractions with which we justify our barbarity.

Moderate Dove Statements:

1. The United States interference in Vietnam has done little good and much harm.
2. There is very little justification for the lives lost in Vietnam.

Mild Dove Statements:

1. The American people should become more aware of the cost of our actions in Vietnam.
2. The disadvantages of our Vietnam policy somewhat outweigh its advantages[18]

Getting research volunteers to study communication processes in this atmosphere was no problem. The investigators ran newspaper ads for participants and had plenty of volunteers. The experimenters put advertisements in the University of Oregon newspapers soliciting students who believed in the Hawk and Dove positions. Those who volunteered to be participants were then presented with questionnaires to make judgments about "how extreme" the statements were. Of course, the participants did not know who wrote the statements.

The results were clear: In the majority of comparisons, the Hawks rated the Dove statements as more extreme than they rated the Hawk statements, and the Doves rated the Hawk statement as more extreme than they rated the Dove statements. If you think of your opponent as an extremist, no wonder you would "contrast away" most of what he says.

The next experiment by these investigators probed this effect further in a particularly powerful test. They asked the participants themselves to create statements representing their own opinion and, tellingly, the opinion of the other side of the issue. To do this, they recruited new groups of partisans and engaged them in statement-writing and statement-judging tasks. Here are the instructions for the first phase:

> We are planning to engage in research concerning attitudes toward the Vietnamese war. We are going to use college students in this research, and we will be asking them to endorse or reject the sorts of statements that college students typically make about the war. We are asking your help in obtaining such statements. Please write four statements that you think would be endorsed by the typical Hawk on campus. . . . Now, please write four statements that you think would be endorsed by the typical Dove on campus.[19]

The point here was to get advocates to represent both ends of the issue, their own and that of their opponents. This study very cleverly gave the ego-involved partisans on either side of the Vietnam War the task of having to understand their own position and the position opposite to theirs by actually writing out those positions. Can involved people do this at all, and, if so, how well can they do it? This was a very stringent test of ego-involvement effects. Can people do a reasonable job of stating their own end of the scale and the opponents' end of the scale, which they dislike and which is one that undoubtedly would be in their latitude of rejection? In our current time (2012), an analogous task would be to have prolife advocates commit themselves to writing statements supporting the prochoice position and prochoice people commit themselves to write prolife statements. You can imagine the mental turmoil if you could actually get them to do the task. Beyond this first step, you would want to find out, if they would agree to do it, what kind of job would they do? Could a partisan Democrat write a reasonable statement of the Republican position, and could a partisan Republican write a reasonable statement about the Democratic position? Could an antidrug advocate support legalization of marijuana? Agreeing to do this task is one level of stress, but we would also want to determine just what kind of job they would do.

The experimenters next recruited new groups of Hawks and Doves to act as judges of these written statements. Of course, the experimenters eliminated any identifying information as to who had written the statements. They asked the participants to review all of these statements and to check off particular statements they agreed with and those which they did not agree. For the sentences with which they rated that they did not agree with, they were additionally asked to indicate why not. For this key judgment, the experimenters provided two reasons for disagreeing: because the statement was too strongly worded or because it was too mildly worded.

To review where the actual method of the study stands at this point: in effect (and I know how this is going to sound!), the experimenters had Hawks reading and responding to Hawk-written statements about the Hawk position, and Doves reading and responding to Dove-position statements written by Doves. But the true innovation of this study was its focus on the rejection process, when people reject statements about socially sensitive issues. This is another angle of approach to the contrast effect. Ego-involved people have much larger latitudes of rejection than they have latitudes of acceptance and the latitude of non-commitment. So additionally this technique answers the following question (and again this will sound tricky . . .): What happens when Hawks respond to Hawk-position statements actually written by Doves, and what happens when Doves read and respond to Dove-position statements written by Hawks? If there is extremizing and polarizing going on in radical speech and radical hearing, the Dawes, Singer, and Lemons study brilliantly set it up for rigorous testing.

The results showed that people actually do not reject as too extreme statements representing their own side of the issue written by people on their own side of the issue. But they clearly rejected as "too extreme" statements of their own position when those statements were constructed by their opponents! Hawks rejected more Dove-written statements about the Hawk position than they rejected Hawk-written statements of that same Hawk position. Conversely, Doves rejected more Hawk-written statements of the Dove side of the issue than they rejected Dove-written statements of their side of the issue. As you might expect from all that has gone on before, both groups of participants showed this tendency to about the same degree. Again, it is not differences in direction of beliefs, but the extremity of beliefs, that is the key to biases in judgments. In short, it is those extremists on the other side who are the problem . . . we assume, naturally, that we ourselves are more moderate.

The question arises: Did Hawks really write too-extreme versions of the Dove position when they thought it up, and did Doves really write too-extreme statements when they conjured up their interpretation of the Hawk side? Exactly where is the bias occurring? Is the distortion inside of the thinking processes in the writers as they try to represent their opponents' viewpoint? Or is it something in just subtle wordings that people who hold to that end of the issue have in mind when they make judgments about their position? Is the bias in our heads, or is it in their heads?

It is important to remember that the Hawks and Doves who were responding to the statements did not know who wrote them, so that obviously biasing information could not "contaminate" their thinking. It appears that the bottom line to these questions is, simply, that we have no way of knowing the exact location in the communication chain at which this extremizing was occurring. What we can tell is that biasing was happening, it was a real thing and the two ego-involved groups of partisan participants rejected and would not endorse even their own side of the issue when they read what their opponents had construed about their side. These data show just how complicated our tolerating other people can get when our thoughts about their beliefs get so biased, if not distorted, by our own personal emotions.

THE "HOSTILE MEDIA" PHENOMENON

Distorting each other's point of view by extremizing it is a very destructive thing for social unity because it just accentuates differences and makes it more difficult to overcome radical hearing's divisiveness. This is basically a "two-party dispute" problem because the extremizing takes place somewhere between opponents and partisans. Moderates are outside that loop and are not heard, so they cannot get to be a party to the dispute. But as with many social problems, the tension caused by two warring parties spreads ripples out into other people and society.

Researchers have shown us that there is yet another form of misunderstanding that infuses radical hearing. This arises when people think that other people who are not directly opposing them but who are neutral or noncommitted on the issue, bystanders in effect, nevertheless do not have a fair and impartial understanding their own position. We know that judgments of truth and fairness are compromised by high levels of partisanship and ego-involvement. If you think that people who should be fair and unbiased about your position are in fact actually biased against you, then certainly that would make agreement with an acceptance of those other people more difficult. It can only heighten tension and tendencies toward rejection such as Dawes, Singer, and Lemons showed. We see this sort of distortion in thinking when we watch people who lose an election blame the media for their loss. In the words of the investigators who discovered and analyzed this effect, Robert Vallone, Lee Ross, and Mark Lepper, there is anecdotal evidence in the "bitter memories of defeated candidates and retired politicians about the 'unfair treatment' they suffered from the press, or denunciations of the media by spokesmen for various interest groups who complain about 'conspiracies' to ignore or distort their concerns."[20]

We need more than anecdotal evidence of course, no matter how compelling, but to see if this effect is a real factor biasing our judgments, the investigators conducted a study to investigate it systematically. To recruit participants, they selected one of the hottest of the hot-button topics at the time, and even now, the Arab–Israeli conflict in the Middle East. The particular focus of the study came from extensive news reports of a massacre of civilians in refugee camps in Lebanon during one of the times of tension between Israel and its neighboring countries. Those news stories became the focus of the study, and the investigators wanted to determine what partisans who had intense feelings about the conflicts would think of news coverage of the conflict.

The investigators recruited Stanford University college students following the "known-groups" method. The students were active members of pro-Arab and pro-Israel student associations. In addition, the experimenters also recruited regular college students who did not identify themselves with either side of the conflict. Before the experiment actually began, the students filled out a brief questionnaire concerning their opinions on the massacre and, specifically, Israel's role in causing it. The responses showed that the Arab group assigned 57 percent of the responsibility to Israel, whereas the pro-Israel students assigned only 22 percent of the responsibility to Israel. Clearly there were biases going on even before the study began.

The investigators had videotaped six segments of the event broadcast by national networks over a period of ten days. They made sure that the newscasts had provided detailed information and significant amounts of film footage, providing vivid information for the participants to judge. Then they asked the students to view the videotapes and then to respond to a series of questions about what they had seen. The questions of interest here are those that assessed perceptions of the fairness and objectivity about the broadcasts.

There were several different ways of detecting any biases. One question dealt with "overall treatment of Israel" in the newscasts. Pro-Arabs rated the newscasts as showing a bias in favor of Israel, and pro-Israel students rated those same newscasts as showing a bias against Israel. Pro-Arab students thought that the news programs applied lower standards to Israel ("excusing Israel when they would have blamed some other country") while pro-Israel students responded just the opposite, applying higher standards to Israel ("blaming Israel when they would have excused some other country"). These perceived biases were generalized to perceptions of the editorial staffs of the news organizations. The participants also guessed that the "personal views" of the editors were opposed to their own views; pro-Arab students believed that the editorial staffs were more pro-Israel while the pro-Israel students believed that those news staffs were pro-Arab.

Throughout all of these data comparisons, the uncommitted students who did not identify themselves as members of either side of the issue did not show any particular patterns of biases in their judgments on these same questions.

I have used the phrase "If you are not with me, then you are against me" several times in this book, and here we see it again, with emotionally involved people estimating the degree of support they can expect from "others." Not very much support, obviously, and their perceived lack of support is directly related to the degree of ego-involvement in the issue generating their upset. Middle-of-the-road opinions are likely to get lost when radical-hearing processes undermine the very grounds on which middle-of-the-road opinions could get to be trusted in the first place. If you think that outsiders are biased in favor of your opponent, why listen to them in the first place?

Vallone, Ross, and Lepper provide a nice extension of their results into other realms of our social divisiveness. Here is their final paragraph:

> Finally, we note that our analysis and the questions it raises may also apply to perceptions of other types of mediation. Whether it is

sports fans' perceptions of referees, spouses' perceptions of family-crisis counselors, or labor and management's perceptions of government arbitrators, even the most impartial mediators are apt to face accusations of overt bias and hostile intent. Such accusations, our analysis suggests, may involve far more than unreasoning and unreasonable wishes for preferential treatment. Rather, they may reflect the operation of basic cognitive and perceptual mechanisms that must be understood and successfully combated if mediation or negotiation is to succeed.[21]

I certainly agree with these authors' pointing to the "basic cognitive and perceptual mechanisms" as topics to be understood. Their discussion of third parties is particularly useful because our lives are filled with "third parties" such as counselors, referees, even our friends and acquaintances when they buffer our relationships with each other. Moderate people, the ones whose voices get lost in these polarized situations, could be looked up to as the best communicators who can provide unbiased information about our conflicts. But in radical hearing we now know that they will not be heard.

CHAPTER 7
THE RADICAL HEARING DIAGNOSTIC TEST

I t is one thing to read about the research on radical hearing. But understanding the techniques and results of research as well as the technical details of how radical hearing operates is different from actually being able to *observe it* in real life. We are familiar with radical speakers; we get exposed to them nearly every day. But getting into a mode for detecting what I call "the technical aspects" of radical hearing is more complicated. Shifting the focus to oneself rather than focusing on the very visible radical speakers takes some effort. We are just not ready to look at our own way of hearing as a possible problem. First, I want to briefly characterize the visible, public, everyday characteristics of radical speakers so that I then can contrast them with the much more subtle characteristics of radical hearers, the audience, among which our social divisiveness has found its home.

Radical hearing is pretty blatant if you know what you are "seeing." You have to learn to listen for the underlying biases and slanted thinking that leads radical hearers to their simple categorizing. And you have to listen for the exaggerated assimilation and contrast principles that underpin their thinking and their undermining of the grounds of the beliefs of their opponents.

First, there is little doubt that radical speakers and their followers, radical hearers, can be highly impressive, commanding figures, quick to reply, sharp at their edges, and sometimes even funny. That makes them engaging, but if you think about what you are hearing, it does not necessarily make them convincing. If you look behind the curtains, you will see the Wizard of Oz, pulling levers, shouting loudly, blowing fire and smoke, scaring everyone. No matter how smart and how verbally dazzling some radical speakers may be, their effects cannot go anywhere if you catch them at their act. But if you go one step further and look at the *judgment categories* of such people, there you will see the limited number of separate distinctions they are making; the tell-tale, two-category, black-and-white thinking; the low thresholds of rejection characteristic of the contrast effect; the high threshold for acceptance; and the low assimilation effect. There may well be a lot of words, but there will not be a lot of categories and important distinctions. Look past the words and find the discernments and comparisons; they will be impoverished in radical speech.

To help you become a good detective for sniffing out radical hearing, I provide here a detective kit of a sort, or a personal Geiger counter to help you pick up its presence and its intensity. In my opinion, we can all do our society a good deed by detecting radical speech and then deliberately not endorsing it. "Power to the people" will be our motto if we can take this step and then make a significant advancement in invigorating our social unity. In chapter 9, I describe ways that the scientific evidence we have available to us can be used for that purpose, but in chapter 10, I describe why it will be so difficult to do so.

In what follows, first I will highlight the main points of radical hearing that we know to be well established by the research. Then I will present my checklist of the key characteristics of radical hearing as we see it in our everyday life.

A REVIEW OF BASIC PRINCIPLES

- There are those who seek to divide their society by speaking and writing and preaching what turn out to be socially divisive ideas. Some people may like what they say, but those people should ask themselves whether they are really willing to endorse that speech and as a consequence see our society split and broken apart by radical speech and its consequences?
- When people are exposed to radical speech, they are faced

with a decision about whether to endorse it as representing their own position or judge it as objectionable. The endorsement process is, then, the critical connection between radical speech and radical hearing. It is based on three linked cognitive processes that I have summarized in what I have called the "CVC" (choice/value/commitment) model, which consists of freely *choosing* to hear and respond to it, the *valuing process* that follows from the act of free choice, and the *commitment* or embedding in the self-concept that follows from the valuing process.

- Endorsement establishes the cognitive foundation of radical hearing. Radical hearing effects are revealed in the *process of judging* the meaning and personal relevance of what one hears. Judgment is the process of discerning and comparing new information against a reference scale. Research has revealed that there are biases and distortion in reference-scale processing. These come from: (1) *assimilation effects*, where a particular stimulus is distorted to seem more similar to an anchorage point, in this case the end points of a reference scale—in essence, assimilation effects damage the judgment process because, a true difference is overlooked or ignored; (2) *contrast effects*, where extreme anchorages on a reference scale make differences appear to be greater that they truly are—new stimuli are judged in a direction opposite to the comparison anchor point and therefore appear more extreme than they truly are.

- The process of judging physical stimuli such as brass weights is fundamentally the same process that is involved in judging more human characteristics such as beauty and someone's attitudes and beliefs. Judgments in both domains reflect our personal reference scale.

- This basic science of judgment processes, discerning and comparing, sets the foundations for later *psychosocial* science of attitudes and opinions. The Thurstone and Chave technique of assessing beliefs about church-related issues revolutionized the translation of basic science for use in the measurement of emotionally involving, hot-button issues.

- Once endorsement of radical speech has occurred, the person's personal scale for judging attitude-relevant issues becomes anchored to a more extreme end of the reference scale. The anchorage points embedded in the person's self-concept provide structure and certainty that mask the ambiguities of judging opinions and statements of beliefs.

- The studies on hot-emotion topics such as national presidential elections reveal that extreme attitudes held by radical hearers shift their perceptions of moderate or neutral statements entirely away from the middle range; this is how radical hearing eliminates moderate judgments. Middle-of-the-road or neutral statements about a highly involving issue position are not "heard" by people who have extreme stands on that issue.

- In other hot-button issues such as pro- and antialcohol and pro- and antiunion issues, more highly committed participants used *fewer* categories (poorer discerning abilities) to make their judgments as compared with more moderate participants, revealing tendencies toward black-and-white, simple, two-category judging among the highly committed participants. Even in those participants who used more categories and superficially appeared to be more open-minded, in fact they still showed significantly more bunching up of statements. Their biased judgment led them to make poorer distinctions among the attitude-relevant statements. Ego involvement leads to less "discerning" and "more crude" comparing when it comes to a person's judgment processes.

- The concept of the "latitudes" is a powerful new technique for giving us a more nuanced, more complex, and more sophisticated view of attitude bias effects. Emotional biases *simultaneously* lead to a larger latitude of rejecting beliefs different from one's own and a tendency to pass judgment on most beliefs, which shows up as a smaller latitude of noncommitment. But moderate, unbiased judges can detect and judge larger numbers of distinctions among different statements of opinions, resulting in larger latitudes of noncommitment. Therefore, moderate people are better able to "see" middle-range and moderate speech than are more strongly ego-involved, committed people.

- Highly "pro" ego-involved partisans at first glance seem to be exactly opposite to highly "anti" people (they endorse attitudes at the opposite end of a judgment scale). In fact, studies show that they are making judgments in exactly the same way; that is, members of both categories display larger latitudes of rejection and smaller latitudes of noncommitment. Both types of extreme radical hearers are judgmentally exactly alike, and they are distinctly different from more moderate, noncommitted, nonpartisan judge. One of the key findings of this entire body of research shows that it is not one's stance, but the extremity of one's stance, that makes the real difference in radical hearing.

- In addition to category judgments, when asked about the extent to which statements about an ego-involving topic are biased or unbiased, fair or unfair, true or false, strong or weak, partisans judge statements endorsing their own side of the issue to be "fair," "unbiased," "true," "strong," convincing arguments, whereas statements at the opposite end are judged to be "unfair," "biased," "not true," and "weak." Logically speaking, these judgments may be one key reason that partisans judge opposite statements into their latitudes of rejection. Discussion of differences cannot be productive in these circumstances because neither side can get traction when this type of biased judgment undermines the foundations and intellectual substance of their respective positions.

- Ego involvement and partisanship leads to *quicker* judgments rather than more deliberative and careful thinking. Ego-involved people process their judgments more rapidly than do noncommitted people. The ego-involved partisans tend to "rush to judgment." No wonder then that emotionally involved people do not genuinely listen to others with different opinions: they do not take the time it takes to truly listen.

- Perhaps not surprisingly, when asked if they would commit themselves to attend meetings about social topics and thus make actual behavioral effort, students were at least twice as likely to agree to make the effort for topics that were personally relevant to them as compared to topics that they considered to be less involving. So actual behavioral commitments work in tandem with ego involvement, increasing the consistency of attitude-behavior linkages.

- When highly ego-involved "pro" and "anti" partisans on the issue of the war in Vietnam were asked to think up and write statements that represented their own sides of the issue and also write statements about the opposite end, the "opponents" who actually held opinions at that opposite end of the issue rated those written statements as too extreme and rejected them. But they did not reject statements about their side of the issue when the statements were written by someone at their same end of the scale. So not only does ego involvement lead to a larger latitude of rejection of the opponent's point of view, it also leads to thinking of (and writing about) that position in such extreme terms that partisans at that position will not accept it.

- Regarding the "hostile media" phenomenon, when partisans are shown newscasts showing clashes of political forces, in this case Arab and Israeli relationships, each side accuses the newscasts of being favorable to their opponent's side and hostile to their own. Thinking that supposedly neutral, outside observers are biased against you removes any reason to listen to them. Again, voices of moderation will not be heard when emotions are high.

- Given all of these findings, it seems that we should never expect radicals and fanatics (in Winston Churchill's description) to change their minds. There is no pressure for them to change because they do not possess the needed categories for judging appropriately the speech they "hear." Instead, the speech, if it does not agree with their extreme positions, is contrasted into the opponent categories that they reject. Radicals and fanatics (the highly ego involved or partisan) simply do not have the middle-of-the-road categories necessary for being able to hear and dispassionately consider more moderate propositions.

APPLYING THOSE BASIC PRINCIPLES TO EVERYDAY LIFE

Now I want to bring these scientific principles together to create a set of criteria that anyone can use for picking out and recognizing radical speech as it is happening in everyday life. Extracting general principles from the science of judgment processes, we can pinpoint actual overt characteristics of radical hearing that we might see in our daily living, such as on our TV, in our newspaper or magazine, at our local grocery store, or in our street as we chat with our neighbors. No particular order of these overt characteristics is implied here, although each of these characteristics is a significant indicator. These are general enough principles that they would apply equally well to any particular hot-button topic and any partisan stand, "pro" or "anti," that someone might adopt as their own personal way of engaging in radical hearing. I have extracted these general principles, which are listed on my website at http://www.radicalhearing.com.

KEY CHARACTERISTICS TO LOOK FOR IN RADICAL HEARING

1. *"Fanaticism."* The most obvious characteristic goes back to our quotation from Winston Churchill: a fanatic is someone who

can't change his mind and won't change the subject. Although this might more directly apply to a radical speaker, it would be a likely description of a radical hearer as well. You will know it when you see it, even if it might be stressful for you to label someone you know with such a label. "Truth in lending" ideas might apply here, even if it is hard to admit.

2. *Two-category, "black and white" thinking.* Tendencies to see the world in terms of "our side" and "the other side" come right out of the research studies on partisanship, and this kind of thinking has been demonstrated repeatedly in people highly ego involved on a topic. And such people seem to have an opinion about everything related to the issue; they have a very small latitude of noncommitment.

3. *Immediate decision-making.* If the person makes up his or her mind quickly whenever the topic comes up, if the person immediately shows a preference with little or no cognitive effort on the topic, then that is a sign of rapid processing, which is a characteristic of partisans and a component of radical hearing.

4. *Behavioral commitment.* If a person devotes a significant amount of time and effort to dealing with an issue that other people find uninteresting, accompanied with an unusual degree of attention to either a "pro" side or an "anti" side of the issue, then we might expect that person to endorse an extreme stand on the issue. Research shows that topics of interest will draw the person into meetings and discussion on a central topic to the person, but noncentral topics will not draw that kind of activist behavior. "Time spent on task" is a concept used by experimental psychologists to think about how a person's behavior is spread across alternatives; when one alternative totally dominates others, that is a key characteristic of radical hearing.

5. *Rejection of moderation.* Moderate, middle-of-the-road positions on a hot-button topic are ignored or given no credibility by radical hearers.

6. *Extremizing* and polarizing the opponent's position, making it more extreme than that opponent would actually state, occurs under conditions of high partisanship.

7. *Perception of hostile others.* Thinking that other people are hostile and biased against one's side of an issue is also a reflection of emotion-based, two-category thinking, by which one concludes that there is only one good side—our side only—with people who believe like we do. At the same time, "we" are surrounded by disbelievers and by opponents and their henchmen such as most members of the media, who have it in for us and can be trusted only to be hostile to our deepest beliefs.

ANOTHER SOURCE OF RADICAL HEARING BIASES

These seven characteristics of radical hearing are largely cognitive, inside the mental workings of the individual's mind. That is where judgment resides and where self-concepts and emotional biases get associated with each other. However, one entire category of biases resides outside the person, and the topic is so central to who we are that it requires special treatment and an entire domain of research all by itself. That domain resides in our *social relations and our social identity.* As an example, someone can be a fan of their local football team or they can be a football *fan*atic. There is a world of difference.

The next chapter explores this minefield of socially based emotional biases that lead us into disunity, divisiveness, and, in one famous case, actual war between otherwise nice, normal, eleven-year-old boys at a summer camp.

CHAPTER 8
OUR SOCIAL RELATIONS JUST MAGNIFY OUR BIASES

Humans are social animals, and whether and how this social nature gets connected with our emotions, biases, and the process of judgment that I have been presenting in this book is an interesting question. There is no surprise that the answer to the question of whether our social nature gets connected with our emotions, biases, and judgment process is Yes, but understanding the complex ways in which this comes about gives us truly significant insights into our current society's divisiveness and polarized discourse. Research shows that social relationships generate forces that actually increase the strength of our biases. So it is a major finding that an additional set of factors creating radical hearing lie outside of the person and in the relationships we experience every day in our social environment. Even more important, though, the ways we experience other people and groups can lead to two-category thinking and tendencies to discriminate against one category or the other *even without* the high levels of emotion that I have described in previous studies. Also, what is new here is that the discerning and comparing judgments happen even when we have virtually *no experience with* "the other."

THE MINIMAL GROUP EFFECT

No one would be particularly surprised if a Republican made disparaging remarks about a Democrat, or if a Palestinian disparaged an Israeli, or if a Christian disparaged a Muslim, or if . . . you know . . . the list goes on and on. This kind of social battle infuses most of the bloody stories of human history. Of course, there are many reasons why these fights occur. Religious differences, economic competition, cultural and ethnic differences, and even our familiar radical speech and radical hearing are key causes of divisions. But what about just *difference* itself?

This question was asked in a remarkable and remarkably simple study by Anne Locksley, Vilma Ortiz, and Christine Hepburn.[1] They used a method now commonly called "the minimal group effect." It could not be any simpler. College students in groups of six appeared for an experiment supposedly studying group interaction. They were presented with slips of paper and told to draw out a slip to see which "group" they were going to be in, either a *Phi* group or a *Gamma* group. Unknown to them, however, all of the slips had the same group label *Phi* on it. So they thought that they themselves were Phis, but they also thought that some of the people in the room were Gammas. Once the drawing had taken place, the experimenters then read to the participants the following instructions:

> You have been given five sets of 100 chips each. You can allocate up to 100 chips to each person in your group and to each person in the other group. You are free to determine how many chips you give to each person, so long as you do not give any person more than 100 chips. Your choice for one person does not have to influence your choice for another person. Do not allocate any chips to yourself.

The participants were then given a set of paper sheets, each having the word *Phi* or *Gamma* typed on it. They were to make their allocations of points by simply writing a number from 0 to 100 on each sheet labeled with a group name. The results showed that the participants chose to make their allocations in this way: on average, the Phis gave the Phis 85 points, but they gave only 64 points to the Gammas. This is a clear example of biased discerning and comparing; the Phis discerned the others as different then discriminated against them. This result can be looked at in two ways. Either the Phis showed "in-group favoritism" or, reworded, they showed "out-group discrimination." The significant point is that the participants discriminated against the out group even though they could not possibly have had any real information about them other than their label. In fact, the participants really did not know anything at all about their own "team members" either. This study even stretches the concept of "team" or group; it was just barely a "group" study. That is where we get the term *minimal group effect*. In fact, the participants had *no rational grounds at all* for making their judgments. The only grounds for making judgments were the labels attached externally by the experimenters. That was enough. The different name automatically made the Gammas "the others," and on those grounds alone they got what they "deserved": discrimination.

The US Supreme Court ruled in 1954 that "separate facilities are inherently unequal," and this study seems to support that argument. The fact that the Phis and Gammas did not really exist except as group labels says a lot about how deeply the mind's discerning process can get biased. I recall vividly that in the '60s, when I was teaching undergraduates, I would run a quick, show-of-the-hands survey on the question: "How many of you hate the Chinese Communists?" A huge majority of the students would raise their hands. I then asked a second question: "How many of you have ever met or talked with a Chinese Communist?" I never saw one hand go up. Times have changed, and it now seems rather absurd, but anti-communism was serious business at the time. But cognitively, a label is a powerful tool for separating people from each other. It is a way to keep people from finding common ground. Even a fake, meaningless label engages deep biases. If you add the perceptions of political and economic threats, then even war against "them" can come to seem logical and justified.

Another study on this same topic extended our knowledge of how far this minimal group effect can go. Jacob Rabbie and Murray Horwitz asked randomly selected samples of Dutch high school students to attend a research session in groups of eight.[2] The students sat at a table with a large partition down the middle, blocking any meaningful interaction between the four students randomly sitting on one side of the partition and the four sitting on the other side. One side of the partition was painted blue, with blue sheets of rating paper and blue ballpoints for the students to use during the study; the other side had green sheets and green ballpoints for participants to use. When the study began, the experimenter came into the room and casually said that he would be addressing the participants as "Blues" or "Greens." He then announced that he had some gifts for them (small, inexpensive radios). But, he explained, he had only four to give away, and he would have to somehow figure out a way to distribute the presents. In one of the conditions, he announced that he would simply flip a coin to decide how to divide them. After flipping the coin, he distributed the cameras to the "winning" side, although it would be a stretch to consider this a contest. After some other activities, the students were asked to rate the other participants on a set of questions assessing their impressions of each other. The ratings sheet had listed on it some descriptive positive and negative adjectives such as "responsible," "considerate," and so forth. These were to be used by each participant to rate all of the other participants. The results were consistent. When they won the prize, Greens rated Greens more positively than they rated Blues, and the Blues rated members of their own group of Blues more favorably than they rated the Greens.

Keep in mind that the groups had been composed randomly. The raters had little, if any, grounds of real knowledge upon which to make their judgments. If you were a participant, you were assigned your group identity merely by which chair on which side of the colored partition you happened to select when you arrived! Just by sitting in a blue environment, participants formed in-group Blue self-labels and subsequently discriminated against the out-group Green members when they rated their impressions of one another. In effect, the participants rated one another only on the grounds of a purely random toss of a coin, a brief introduction, and the color labels used by the experimenter and made obvious by colors in the experimental arrangements. The experimenter did not show favoritism or try to harm one particular group to the advantage of the other. It was all just chance. Rationally, logically, there were no grounds for feeling pride at one's superiority over another or disgust or anger over being treated unfairly, which are some of the usual candidates for social divisiveness. Interestingly, being a winner of the small radios or being a loser did not make a difference in this pattern of in-group favorability/out-group denigration. Both winning and losing groups discriminated in their evaluative ratings of each other to the same degree, so winning and losing was not the key factor. Note that there was no history of ethnic conflict; no radical speakers trying to stir up divisiveness; no economic, religious, or social competition; and no "Commie" labels.

Although this particular study was conducted in Holland, the results are directly relevant to understanding a core component of the historical development of American ethnic and racial experiences. Just being different in skin color or group label is enough to cause discrimination. It is a natural function of our mental life. But our social relations have added ingredients: negativity, hostility, overt aggression. These are the downside of a discerning and comparing mind. The following quotation by Senator George Aiken of Vermont neatly ties up the essence of this unfortunate tendency: "If we were to wake up some morning and find that everyone was the same race, creed, and color, we would find some other causes for prejudice by noon."[3]

These studies show the ease with which we can come to discriminate against other people. We do it by categorizing them as different from us and then treating members of that category in negative ways. That would seem to be just another extension of what we already know about judgment processes, discerning and comparing. But these research studies show that there is more than just the cognitive process of judging. One of the key components of out-group discrimination is the implied competition or threat that we perceive when we are dealing with people who are not "us," people who are not part of our "we." In radical-hearing terms, they are not in our latitude of acceptance and they are likely to be pushed into our latitude of rejection. Again, if you are not for us, on our side, then you must be against us, on the "other side." This is another manifestation of the two-category, black-and-white thinking that accompanies discerning and comparing.

What remains to be analyzed is how much *competitive motivations* get involved in such judgments. Dealing with people is more complex than dealing with their ideas and their statements of their beliefs. And now we are at a more realistic, if not a more vivid, level of social reality because we are dealing with the actual presence of others rather than just statements about the range of opinions on an issue. There may have been at least a modicum of competitiveness implied in the sharing of points in the study by Locksley and her colleagues, and certainly there must have been such in winning and losing in the Rabbie and Horwitz study. When the students in the Rabbie and Horwitz study saw their "enemies" getting the desirable radios by the toss of a coin, they surely must have experienced a very real sense of competitiveness, along with an inevitable sense of frustration and loss. This is where the dynamic, motivational aspects of our social relations when discerning and comparing start functioning, as I shall show next in some examples from our daily living.

THE SOCIAL DANGER OF SPORTS

If people have some sort of natural group identity that they regard as part of their self-concept, then the discerning and comparing processes follow that lead and get us into situations of out-group discrimination. The fact that this is socially based has the effect of providing even stronger grounds for divisiveness and discrimination. The classic example would be sports. Sports teams are clearly distinguishable on a number of grounds, including voluminous publicity and marketable items distinguishable by the team label and, perhaps subtly, team colors (remember Blues and Greens).

With an identifiable history of team activities supported by fan loyalty, there comes a process of self-identification in the public ("I'm a Dallas Cowboys fan," or "I'm a Sox fan"). That is all well and good. But these identities and this biased thinking can come to the fore if there is a competitive situation of "us" versus "them."

This history brings about its biasing effects in two ways. There is the usual self-identification of fans who wear team colors, attend sporting events, read about their sports heroes, watch them on TV, and so forth. The flip side of this is hostility toward the opponents; that is, the raucous slurs and the denigrating comments thrown at the opponents. Long before the actual contest begins, the mere presence of an upcoming battle is sufficient to get the emotions going.

Although stress from losing can actually have positive effects in stimulating us to greater accomplishments, when it arises from perceived differences between individuals and groups, it can have an emotional biasing effect on judgment. You will recall that in chapter 1 I established the basic distinction in radical speech, the distinction between *radical-supporting speech* and *radical-attacking speech*. One can be an extreme sport fan or an extreme political radical, ego-involved, proclaiming loudly the glory of one's favorite sports team, prized automobile, or hairstyle. That kind of speech, while possibly a bit irritating to the rest of us, has no damaging or harmful effects on the way we live our lives; we can choose to let it go by. But the second category of radical speech is much more damaging. When radical speech becomes radical-attacking speech, it can easily arouse anger and hostility among the people who are its target. To be attacked almost inevitably requires retaliation, and then the spiral of attack and counterattack can become virtually endless.

Human history is written with the blood of innocent and sometimes not-so-innocent participants in these spirals of "getting back at them." In this sense, we find again that the cognitive processes of individuals caught up in these hate-filled situations demonstrate the biases that result from excessive emotional upset. The causes, though, to make my main point in this chapter, are *social*. The perception "different from me" is key to eliciting discrimination against the "other."

To some degree team loyalties may be stimulating, acting as harmless daily diversions. But they are not always harmless. The notorious behavior of British soccer fans who deliberately seek out enemies so that they can engage in battles and wars during soccer games is well known. This has been going on for over a hundred years, and intentional destructiveness is by now the norm of this "harmless diversion" we call a game of soccer. Lest we be dismissive of this peculiarly British phenomenon, our local news often reports on nice, friendly fathers and mothers who batter each other or the referees over some perceived infraction on the field of competition. Obviously, it is really not a very large step to go from "fan" to "fanatic."

What is important to know about this kind of all-too-human characteristic is that there is a subtle difference in how people's self-identities get drawn into the hot-button emotions that result from this kind of process. The hidden ingredient is competition itself. Sports, as an organized social activity, is, of course, based largely on competition, but there are two types of competition, only one of which is connected with destructive, aggressive discrimination against other people. In single-actor sports such as archery, golf, and skeet shooting, there is mostly what the psychologist David McClelland calls "competition against a standard of excellence." No matter how much you may wish to be better than your opponent, you are really competing against such things as accuracy (archery), par (golf), time (track), and so on. We know that competing against other people improves performance when compared to performing alone; this is the so-called *social-facilitation* effect. Note, though, that there is no direct, deliberate attempt to harm the performance of the opposition. And here you can see impressive camaraderie, hand shaking, and warm hugging to congratulate the winner. Why can't we all live that way?

The second type of competition is where destructive interpersonal forces become engaged. Fighting the competition to better them and win the game generates an entirely different type of competitive motivation. To weaken the opponents, to degrade their ability to perform, to harm them, becomes the most destructive part of competitive performance. In football, "taking out" the quarterback is considered a laudatory act. In basketball, one deliberately breaks the rules to gain an advantage—taking a penalty point for stopping the opponent from scoring is considered to be a valuable part of a player's skill set. The difference between being competitive and being destructive is a thin line, and it is that distinction that gives special meaning to the "social" component of radical hearing. We call them "games," but from this perspective the word takes on a sort of surreal meaning. Frustration and anger as a result of losing is inherent in any situation in which there can only be one winner. There *has* to be a loser; it's locked in, except for occasional ties, which are as unsatisfying as they are rare. Extra playing time is allowed for that outcome, indicating the apparent need for resolution in a condition of uncertainty (from a cognitive-structure perspective).

This sense of losing is inherent in any situation in which there can only be one winner. This type of situation is called "the zero sum game" effect. The effect works this way: the sum of the winnings of one side minus the losses of the opponents on the other side adds to zero. In such a situation, there has to be a winner and there has to be a loser, and of course no one wants to be a loser. This type of situation is the heart of competitive athletics, for instance. The emotional ups and downs of such games are immediately obvious in the public displays of joy and happiness in the faces of the winners and the downcast, quiet agony shown by losers. Worse, though, are the outbursts of recriminations, anger, hostility, and aggression of those who lose the contest.

Psychologists launched a major wave of research studies on the connection between frustration and aggression following the publication of *Frustration and Aggression* by John Dollard, Leonard Doob, Neal Miller, Hobart Mower, and Robert Sears.[4] The authors presented a model of the mind whereby an organism experiences frustration when its movement toward achieving a desired or expected goal is hindered or blocked. The model was originally stated in a strong form: frustration always leads to aggression, and aggression always results from frustration. Later investigations qualified it considerably, but the core idea continues to dominate thinking about how animals and humans show the distinct pattern of this linked relationship. One major qualification is that if there is a threat of punishment should the organism show aggression, then that threat tends to lower the chances of an aggressive response. The model posits that the motivated drive is still there, but it gets "displaced," causing the aggression to be directed at a substitute. Kicking the family dog when coming home after a bad day at work is a familiar cliché, but it may well have a kernel of truth.

In fact, and much more seriously, Joseph Hepworth and Stephen West analyzed data on economic distress and frustration and social hostility against out groups in American history, especially the American south.[5] They did this by calculating the statistical relationship between cotton prices and lynching of black people in the American south in the years between 1882 and 1930. They found a significant direct relationship; as economic conditions worsened, the frequency of lynching increased. There seems to be a strong drive to retaliate against those who frustrate us. But this study shows that aggression is not always directed at the source of frustration. In this case, the source of frustration was the commodities traders who set the cotton prices or perhaps even the ironclad laws of supply and demand. Instead, aggression was directed against black people who had no role in setting the price of cotton. In effect, they could not have been the source of the frustration; they were themselves as impoverished and as powerless as the white aggressors. But there was a distinctive ingroup-outgroup distinction in which skin color no doubt played a significant role in fostering the aggressiveness. Displacement of this sort shows the power of visible stigma and group labels, which are readily available "heuristics" for the shortcut thinking processes I described earlier, in chapter 2.

Return for a moment to the "Blues" and "Greens" study conducted by Rabbie and Horowitz. Their choice of color as the distinguishing feature of their two "groups" of participants is particularly noteworthy for what it says about discerning differences. An extensive literature on juvenile and criminal gangs has developed, attempting to analyze why and how such social groups arise and, more particularly, how it is that they become aggressive and often law breaking. Perhaps the paradigm example of this is the Bloods and Crips of Los Angeles, two large-scale, well-organized groups of young males. They are discussed in the book *Juvenile Gangs* by Herbert Covey, Scott Menard, and Robert Franzese.[6] As with many other such gangs, the individual members went to great lengths to distinguish themselves from outgroups and give themselves a strong sense of self-identity as group members. In reference to our current discussion, both groups initially were particularly noted for their colors: Bloods insisted on wearing the color red on their hats and clothes, while the Crips, apparently in response, were noted for wearing the color blue. So here we have reds and blues rather than blues and greens, but we are now in a completely different realm from the one encountered by the experimental participants in the Rabbie and Horowitz study. In analyzing the "gang mentality" of such groups, Tim Delaney[7] has noted the central feature of group life: the individual members demanding respect from others, combined with the high priority placed on retaliation and revenge for any actual or perceived infractions against the image of the home group. Regarding this aspect of the gang mentality, he states that

> consistent style of dress among members of a gang is another behavior that unifies the group. . . . The "we" feeling is overtly displayed by wearing the same colors or style of clothes. The category of "they"—the rival gangs—becomes easily identifiable because "they" will be sporting different colors or styles. The designation of one group as a "they" group implies that confrontations between the two are inevitable. Since conflict is inevitable for gang members,

they must be willing to fight. Physical strength and prowess in the field of battle are behaviors worthy of automatic respect among gang members.[8]

INTERGROUP HOSTILITIES: THE ROBBERS CAVE STUDY

We do not have information about the degree to which the participants in the minimal-group studies actually felt any personal stress over competition; certainly there was no competition implied in the researchers' instructions to the participants to just divide up one hundred theoretical points. The experimenters did not even ask any direct questions about those feelings. So the logical question about genuine competitiveness inherent in these minimal social conditions had to be answered by a different type of study, the goal of which was to deliberately induce a competitive motivation and then see how this would play out in intergroup relationships. It happens on sport fields all the time; indeed, in the world of group sports (as opposed to single-competitor sports) coaches try to induce a maximally competitive motivation in the players. From what we have said so far in this chapter, coaches have a judgmental process in their favor: group-on-group situations enhance out-group discrimination.

The core issue in many forms of intergroup hostility would seem to be biasing that arises from the presence of competitive motivations, the desire to beat the enemy. Muzafer Sherif and his wife, Carolyn Sherif, along with their colleagues O. J. Harvey, Jack White, and Robert Hood, designed an experiment on frustration and ego-involvement to study judgmental biases in a competitive group interaction. A complete report of the study is contained in their book titled *Intergroup Cooperation and Conflict: The Robbers Cave Experiment.*[9] This classic experiment is generally considered to be the closest thing to experimentally controlled war ever devised. It deserves extra discussion.

Of most interest to us here is what happens when two groups come into contact under conditions of competition. Studying this requires direct experimental manipulation of the spirit of competition and observation of whether aggression arises from it. The study was designed to be an experimental test of how intergroup tensions can be reduced or eliminated. Investigators arranged conditions in which groups could form, then they arranged conditions to create and observe interactions between those groups. Finally, they arranged conditions to test models of how intergroup tensions could be eliminated.

The investigators spent an entire year selecting as participants boys who had no known history of adjustment problems or delinquency, were in the middle socioeconomic class, were not from broken homes, and were in the upper half of scholastic standing. The experimenters canvassed local schools and interviewed teachers, ministers, and of course the parents and the children themselves. The boys were as "normal" and as healthy as could be found. The researchers wanted to ensure as much as possible that any group structure or intergroup problems would arise as naturally as possible from the conditions of the interactions themselves, and not external causes.

Stage I: Ingroup Formation

The twenty-two eleven-year-old boys were invited to participate in what looked like a summer camp experience, but it was run in every detail by experimenters acting as camp counselors. It was sct in a remote Boy Scout campground and run exactly as a summer camp would be run, with camping and hiking experiences, a special swimming hole, a communal dining hall, and so on. The boys were divided into two evenly matched groups and assigned to separate transportation groups to be taken to the summer-camp setting, one bunch leaving for the campus on a bus in the morning and the other in the afternoon, ensuring that they did not see each other or even know of each other. Once at the Robbers Cave State Park (in Oklahoma), they were located in widely separated areas of the camp and engaged in normal camping experiences for nearly a week, during which their ingroup formation processes were observed unobtrusively by the experimenters/counselors.

Careful attention was paid to how in-group membership and self-identification processes evolved as the boys, initially strangers to each other, came to know each other and form group roles and structures. In fact, the boys spontaneously developed clear group identifications. One group spontaneously labeled themselves the "Rattlers" following an accidental encounter with a snake. The other group came to identify themselves as "Eagles" from the spotting of a local avian specimen. These names were proudly stenciled on T-shirts, and group flags were flown from the flagpole at the camp baseball diamond. This is a critical moment, when the "I" or "me" becomes attached to "our flag" or "our camp" and "I" becomes "I'm an Eagle." This is the core of the socialization process, and it brings with it emotional commitment and intense feelings of dedication. Military training and boot camp experiences are constructed for exactly these same reasons.

Stage II: Intergroup Conflict

When the researchers decided that two well-structured, tight-knit groups had evolved naturally, they instituted the second phase, the phase devoted to studying the intergroup contact process and then any subsequent group interactions. This initiating event occurred when one group member spied a boy who was not part of his own group. This led the boys in the group to an immediate sense of alarm about a stranger in "our campgrounds" and a hot desire to find out more about him (remember my earlier discussion of how the mind needs to eliminate uncertainty). You need to be alert if there are enemies around. Apparently it takes very little to find an enemy.

Later, when it was announced by one of the counselors that another group was in the vicinity, an immediate call to challenge them to a game of baseball arose spontaneously in the boys. At this point the counselors announced that there would be a tournament involving a series of competitive activities, including several baseball games, several tug-of-wars, tent pitching, and a touch football. The winning team would be awarded a trophy, medals would be given for the individual team members, and each member of the winning team would get a four-bladed scout knife, a highly desirable prize.

A hint about how things were going to go came early. As I noted, the boys wanted to compete with "the others" the moment they became aware that the others were present. The initial contest of the series was the perfect American example, a baseball game played on the local diamond. The Rattlers won, amid much razzing and cat-calling on both sides. After the first baseball game, the first tug-of-war was held, again with the Rattlers winning. That afternoon the losing Eagles tore down and burned the flag of the winning Rattlers. This insult to their group label led the Rattlers in turn to steal the Eagles' flag, causing hostilities to further escalate. As the contests continued over the next several days, so did the hostilities. Raids on the cabins of the other team became carefully planned wartime events. Joint meals together at the camp dining hall, what might otherwise have been pleasant social experiences, became occasions for pushing and shoving, more verbal hostilities and derogatory name calling, and, as you might expect, food fights. These jousts became so vicious that the counselors eventually had to keep the groups from arriving at the mess hall at the same time. Eventually, mere intergroup contact itself became so much like war that the boys were devoting nearly all of their free time to planning and carrying out raids against their enemies; time that could have been productively used for learning outdoor skills was redirected and devoted almost exclusively to war planning and execution. By the end of the six-day period planned for studying the intergroup contacts, the hostilities had gotten so intense that the experimenters decided to terminate contacts between the groups entirely, and the next two days were used for cooling off and engaging in pleasurable in-group camping activities.

Stage III: Reducing Intergroup Conflict

At this point in the experiment, the investigators moved into the planned third phase of the study, the implementation of a series of intergroup contact activities specifically designed to eliminate the hostilities between the groups. As with the other parts of the study, the trick was to make these contact experiences seem to be entirely natural occurrences that might routinely occur in a summer-camp setting. These activities required the boys from either group to cooperate with their opponents in order to achieve their own goals. The goals could not be achieved without the required cooperation. Members of both groups were asked to use the tug-of-war rope, previously an instrument of competition, to pull an apparently broken-down truck carrying needed food supplies. They worked together to repair the "broken" camp water system when they were hot and thirsty. They had to cooperate with members of the other group to share expenses so that they could bring to the camp a desirable film (*Treasure Island*). They cooperated in an effort to straighten out camping supplies that had somehow become mysteriously jumbled. They prepared a joint meal from a common supply of food. And they jointly took a mutually satisfying trip across the state border for an additional camping experience.

All of these activities, potentially abhorrent because they required cooperation with the enemy, lost their venom as the value of necessary cooperation became obvious to the boys. In the language of the experimenters, the success of this third phase of the experiment was due to the introduction of *superordinate goals*, which are *goals that are desirable for all participants but are not achievable without the cooperation of all.* The introduction of these goals over the course of a week resulted in complete elimination of intergroup hostilities. Gradually, friendships between individual boys formed across group boundaries to such an extent that the lines formerly separating the boys into warring camps dissolved and the group labels ceased to mark useful distinctions (discriminations). The ultimate test of the success of these experiences was shown when, at the end of the third phase, the main camp counselor asked the group members whether two busses should be ordered to take the boys back home or one bus would be sufficient. The boys unanimously voted for one bus.

This amazing experiment created from scratch some of the critical components of the evolution of intense intergroup hostility. It then successfully implemented techniques that were effective in eliminating that hostility. The sociologist Lewis Coser has described this experiment as showing that intergroup hostilities can indeed be removed by the active pursuit of superordinate goals.[10] But he explicitly added that pursuing such goals may well come at the cost of dissolving group boundaries and their associated ego-involvements built up around the sense of group membership. This experiment has lessons that are applicable to helping us foster common purpose in our presently divided and polarized society. We may end up dissolving some of the artificial social boundaries that our minds and their ego-involvement have created for us.

THE MENTAL DYNAMICS OF GROUP MEMBERSHIP AND GROUP IDENTITY

This model of intergroup relations involves an intriguing melding of the social level of group interaction with identity processes inside the self-concepts of the boys. There are important but subtle connections here. One of the models of how the self-concept that people develop becomes identified with their social relationships was initially investigated by sociologists Manford Kuhn and Thomas McPartland.[11] They developed a technique to measure what people thought of themselves—literally, "their selves." To do this, they created the so-called "I am . . ." test. The test consists of twenty incomplete sentence stems. These are presented to respondents in a printed list with twenty numbered sentence stems. Each sentence stem begins with this phrase, "I am . . ." and the instructions are for the person to complete the sentence. This is a wide-open, unstructured task, and that is deliberate. In responding to the stems, the individual has to look inside and find the key labels that define his or her conceptualization of who he or she is.

The subtle but important part of how people respond to this task and what it reveals about them is the *order of descriptions* that people list. The first few descriptive phrases that they come up with most quickly are the most prominent in people's thinking about themselves. And the key finding is that the first descriptions listed are almost invariably *social descriptions*; that is, these first, off-the-top-of-the-head descriptions refer to social roles and positions in society. After that, more idiosyncratic or personal descriptions occur, but these are further down the list and therefore less central to the true self-concept. Here are some typical descriptions that occur first in the listings: "I am . . . a mother"; "I am . . . a husband"; "I am . . . a Baptist"; "I am . . . a Democrat." Further down the list are such personal terms as "I am . . . happy" or "I am . . . a pretty good student."

These types of responses give us an insight into how it is that the labels "Rattler" and "Eagle" became so important to the boys in the summer camp, and how those identifications fueled the high degrees of hostility that arose among the boys. The self adopts the group norms and standards of behavior into which it is born and develops; this is the principle factor in socializing children. As they grow up, children incorporate the norms and standards of the social environment in which they develop. The term researchers use for this process is *socialization,* or *interiorization,* as I described in chapter 2. These are names for the process whereby the physical and social environment initially external to the child gets internalized as the child's own concept of who he or she is. In the Robbers Cave experiment it was shown that when the group is under the threat of losing a competition, so is the self. The Rattler "selfs" fought valiantly against the Eagle "selfs" with the goal of winning for their group the highly desired four-bladed knives. In fact, the Kuhn and McPartland data support the general model of self proposed by one of the founders of American psychology (and philosophy): William James. James proposed the following definition for the concept of the "social" self: "A man has as many social selves are there are individuals who recognize him and carry an image of him in their mind. . . . [W]e may practically say that he has as many different social selves as there are distinct groups of persons about whose opinion he cares."[12]

That is exactly what Kuhn and McPartland found. We define our "self" predominantly in terms of our social connections. At the beginning of the Robbers Cave study, the boys certainly would not have thought up and adopted such labels as Rattlers and Eagles to describe themselves, but over the course of the first few days, the close interactions and mutually satisfying relationships they had with their teammates led them to adopt a brand-new social identity. These labels became infused with emotional commitment and deep personal meaning, as one would expect when one comes to identify oneself. They drew rattlesnake pictures on their T-shirts, in one case, and a soaring eagle in the other, and those identities became loaded with emotional meaning. This became clear when they were challenged by the competition. After the first tug-of-war competition, which the Rattlers won, an Eagle found the Rattler's flag on the baseball field and burned it. Hostility arose right off the bat, hostility directed at the alien "other." The next day, the Rattlers came with a planned course of action, or perhaps a better word would be vengeance. They seized the Eagle's flag and ostentatiously threw it into the dirt and stepped on it. Along with this, of course, came scuffling and bitter name calling, and things escalated into further acts of war over the following days. Nothing is more infuriating than the desecration of one's flag; it represents the ultimate insult to the self. Once the self-definition became threatened by the formation of in-group and out-groups, the fate of the intergroup competition process was sealed. When radical speakers can get people to identify themselves as one "sort" of person, such as "we are the patriots" or "we are the true Christians" or "we are the future of the Fatherland," the logical consequences of radical hearing get played out almost inevitably.

Generally speaking, when people engage in aggressive and discriminatory activities, as these boys did, the average person might want to say that the hostilities were due to the "aggressiveness" of the individual boys. That would be explaining the battle as being due to something about the character of individuals or even their innate biologically based drives. But that is not at all the model that the Sherif team tested in their Robbers Cave study. The types of explanations that may be used to account for the intense aggression can be illustrated by considering what at first glance seems to be a similar case. I am referring to the graphic story *Lord of the Flies* by William Golding[13] (and the 1963 film adaptation). In this story, a group of seemingly normal boys are deserted on a remote island, and slowly but inexorably they evolve into two warring factions. Violence and even pursuit for murder become group norms. Death is averted only when an adult external authority figure in the form of a naval commander comes onto the scene and returns rationality to the situation.

I do not know if Golding had read about the Robbers Cave study before he began writing his story, but the similarities are interesting. A careful reading or viewing of this compelling drama reveals that it follows a model in which the hostilities between the in-group and out-group are the result of the boys' deep-lying, innate aggressiveness. Although at first the boys respond to the leadership and rational coping directives of the most "rational" of the boys, Ralph, they eventually fall into hostility and even murderous war by shifting their loyalties to the most aggressive boy, Jack. Even Ralph, the most rational of the boys, eventually succumbs to the pleasure of killing an animal, and he barely survives attack himself.

The Robbers Cave study is an entirely different matter. Remember that the boys were initially selected to be "normal" in all important ways; there was no evidence of any form of pathology, social adjustment problems, history of family problems, or any of the other usual suspects brought up to account for social aggression and divisiveness. The experimenters ruled out that sort of explanation in their experimental design. Instead, this experiment shows very compellingly that the outcome may be best understood *not* at the level of the individual person. The outcome was a natural product of the *social* situation, an emergent property of a collection of people who think in terms of "we" and "they." Competition with the other group of campers just served to increase divisive emotions arising out of their separateness. It is in the social situation itself, and simple two-category thinking of "us" versus "them" that is the key factor. This is an entirely natural, perhaps inevitable outcome of the *perception of difference itself.* Once the boys separated into visibly distinct groups, the discrimination between "us" and "them" became mentally embedded. The social-interaction situation only magnified the "discerning and comparing" fundamentals of the judgment process. The hostilities toward the out-group worsened when there was competition for resources (a conch shell in Golding's story). To capture the prize psychologically requires removal of the competitor, with all of the emotional and self-identity baggage that doing so implies.

HOW THE SELF COULD BE RESPONSIBLE FOR RADICAL HEARING

Recall that as the Robbers Cave boys initially met and came to know each other, they evolved into a well-structured group. Both sets of boys did this as a natural evolution of their daily experiences, and as group structures arose, so did an identifiable group name and self-identity for each boy. This is the interiorization process I discussed earlier. The group labels were not at all imposed by the researchers, nor did the researchers even suggest anything along those lines. This was all freely chosen behavior, which is a key to adopting the commitments and rigidity of beliefs that I described in chapter 2.

The close identity of the individual boys and their group identity became a key ingredient in how they interacted with each other within each group and, especially, how they interacted with and came to fight "that other group." The very name of the opponent group elicited hate and derision in the boys. They fought valiantly for their group to win because it was important to their *selfs* to win. This is a key finding for a lot of reasons. It reflects a process of self-identity that naturally arises in our daily interactions with "other people." In judgment language, the self-label becomes a major *anchorage* as people judge the acceptability or objectionability of other people. By contrasting the "enemy" away from the self, the inexorable path toward intergroup hostility was set.

The takeaway message is that people who endorse radical speech do so not only because they are emotional about the particular attitude subject to which they are committed, but also because of the self-concept they have developed. Radical hearing and the endorsement of radical political, religious, or social positions is based on what we think of ourselves, literally, *our selves.*

Calling themselves "Nazis" must have felt very elating and stimulating to the German citizens who joined the Nazi Party, just as Russians who joined the Communist Party must have felt empowered by their membership. The same goes for Democrats, Republicans, liberals, Girl Scouts, Cubs fans, Baptists, Catholics, Canadians, Americans, and so forth. The list of group distinctions that humans have created for themselves is nearly infinite. When social relations get so poisoned that "we Christians" have to oppose "those Muslims," or when "we Muslims" have to eliminate "those infidels," then we all should acknowledge the dangers of how the emotions arising from social identities lead us into destructive patterns of thinking and behaving. All of these processes show how difficult it will be for us to heal our habits of polarized thinking. The final chapter describes some principled ways in which this might be accomplished.

CHAPTER 9
SEVEN BASIC PRINCIPLES FOR RESTORING OUR UNITY

People are adaptable and societies are adaptable. Although our own society currently is under attack from radical speakers who want to divide us from each other, our social relations will continue to evolve, crippled or not. We have always had extremists and radicals pushing for their point of view. As Churchill said, they won't change their minds and they won't change the topic. So if any unifying forces are to be found, it has to be among individuals who might be able to reject radical speech when they are exposed it. That is why this book has been focused on understanding the mental processes of those people who actually endorse that speech and accept it into their own ways of viewing the world. Endorsing and internalizing radical speech is a big step, both for the individual and for the rest of us.

Social divisiveness becomes established when people become radical hearers. Dealing with one another, even someone whose beliefs we dislike, has to be an open and flexible process. Above all, it has to be a less emotional process. How are we going to find better ways of accommodating each other's differences? Similarities are no problem! We can try to use our common sense and hope that seat-of-the-pants guesses about ways to do this might work, but I suggest that we follow a more disciplined, informed, and principled set of directives. This book has discussed some of the key principles of judgment when radical hearing has become a way of life for people who endorse radical speech. In reviewing the relevant research, I have found seven principles that offer us the best way out of our current societal divisiveness.

1. Radical-Supporting versus Radical-Attacking Speech

The first step toward creating a new sense of social unity is to understand fully the distinction I made in chapter 1 concerning the differences between two kinds of radical speech: radical-supporting speech *and* radical-attacking speech. If someone is speaking of something for which they have a great liking or high personal enthusiasm, then broadcasting their feelings about it is understandable, perhaps interesting, maybe even informative and helpful. No one likes a braggart, except maybe the bragger, but it is not fundamentally an important social problem. We can just ignore the person and the radical speech, and this will not have any important personal or social consequences. I suspect that this type of situation happens to every TV viewer who gets up and leaves the room when some advertiser touts its product. When a political candidate touts his or her great prowess as a problem solver, that is expected of politicians, and what the candidate says may or may not make the news. But there is always the looming specter that radical supporting speech can shade over into something more destructive. However, if the candidate then moves to radical attacking speech, denigrating the opponent, warning the country of our mortal danger should the opponent win, we are into radical-attacking speech. Therein lies the danger: retaliation is virtually assured. With retaliation comes the cycle of charges, countercharges, misunderstandings, and hardened, uncompromising radical stances. People who attack other people's beliefs are inevitably going to receive "pay back" in the cyclical form of similar attacks. You have to wonder what people expect to gain from being the instigator? It clearly can be lucrative; it draws crowds and that draws big money. So here I am casting radical-attacking speech as a social phenomenon, with a cycle of extremism that begets extremism from others. Who gains from this type of cycle? One thing seems clear from both a historical perspective and a reading of the research literature: attitudes and beliefs do not get changed under attack or under conditions of high emotional involvement; in fact, they get hardened that way. And voices of moderation get drowned out. How could they be heard?

Be alert to the presence of radical-attacking speech. Check the intentions of the speaker. If the intent is to harm the target of the speech rather than support the speaker's own point of view, the useless cycle of charge and countercharge may get going. Society does not gain from endless attacking speech.

2. Watch Out for the Endorsement Process

Radical speech is everywhere. Highly public figures are paid millions to spread it, and an eager media keeps it going. But it can have its effects only if members of the public listen to it, attend to it, and adopt it as their own stand, their own personal attitude. Then it gets embedded in that person's personal reference scale for judging their world. External radical speech evolves into internal radical hearing. I described this in my CVC model (choice/valuing/commitment), which I described in chapter 2. If that connection could be broken, if people would not assume that what radical speakers are saying is relevant to their own personal lives, then radical-hearing effects would not be established into their self-concept. In this sense, what a radical speaker communicates may seem interesting, relevant, perhaps even true, but that does not mean that any particular person, you or me, has to personally adopt the aggressiveness, divisiveness, disregard, and denigration of fellow citizens that is the hallmark of radical-attacking speech. But exposure can be circumvented and biasing effects can be avoided if we keep extreme statements from lodging on our own personal scales of judgment. Break the CVC cycle. The key is to make that extreme speech personally irrelevant for one's own personal judgment processes.

Summarizing: Improving Our Public Discourse—Principle Number Two

Don't become a radical hearer. If you can see radical speech as irrelevant to your own personal standards and you can refuse to endorse it, then it cannot bias and distort your own judgment scale.

3. Keep Cool

We know that emotions bias our judgment processes. They cause us to develop two-category, black-and-white thinking that encourages us to miss important distinctions and fine-grained understandings of what other people are saying. Emotions cause our latitudes of acceptance to shrink such that we cannot accept what other people are saying, including moderate statements that might otherwise be helpful for establishing and maintaining harmony. Emotional biasing increases our latitude of rejection, making us reject as unacceptable a large portion of what other people say. You can miss important thoughts and ideas that way. Cutting off ideas that come from someone else because you do not like to hear them is seldom a productive way to go. Recall the dangers of confirmation bias, where we have a strong tendency to expose ourselves only to information on our side of the issue and to actively avoid being exposed to opposite points of view.

The founders of the American government were diverse in many ways, and they often disagreed about what would be an ideal form of government. The results of their disputes and disagreements are a fascinating melding of many different ideas, but by "getting along," they created a hugely successful and enduring form of government. We should try to repeat their success. We should not let it get torn down by radical speakers and their perhaps inadvertent collabora- tors, radical hearers. I say "inadvertent" to give them the benefit of the doubt, but perhaps I should say deliberate collaborators.

Since the research shows that the problem is that our emo- tions color our judgments, there is one simple answer. The answer? Reduce the emotions. At my website, http://www.radicalhearing. com, I suggest that one can adopt a condition of mindfulness such that one objectively listens to what other people are saying, while carefully but coolly observing one's own reactions to what is being said. Sure, no one wants to listen to what one hates, but listening is a powerful tool for learning and understanding. Hate and disliking are poisonous influences on our thinking processes, but, even worse, they degrade our well-being. To keep clean of these influences, cool and rational listening is a strong antidote.

Psychologists have explored ways in which we can reduce the harmful effects of negative thinking and emotional biasing. Such clinician/researchers as Jon Kabat-Zinn[1] and Stephen Hayes[2] have melded traditional Eastern Buddhist thinking and spiritual contemplation techniques with clinical practice to create "mindful awareness" (MA) therapeutic techniques. These techniques are useful for teaching people how to suspend their immediate judgments and quick reactions to their experiences. Through a contemplative, calm awareness of one's emotional reactions, a person is able to suspend disruptive automatic negative feelings and thoughts about their experiences. Although these techniques have not been applied to political or religious conflicts like the ones I have discussed in this book, this kind of approach seems to be a promising avenue for creating a powerful antidote to the infections of radical hearing. You may recall my example of the YouTube "debate" between Bill O'Reilly and Rep. Barney Frank. There simply cannot be any creative solutions to problems when hot emotions are so coloring our interactions that even listening to the other person is blocked. When the other person can't even be heard, accepting what they have to say is impossible.

Even without formal therapeutic treatment, anyone can exercise personal control and self-mastery by cutting out the emotions in their discourse. People can tune out just about anything if they are motivated to do so. Turn off the TV; spend that time doing something more creative than boiling in the hate and frustration of turning fellow citizens turned into objects of your hate. If there were public and consistent attempts by religious, political, and educational leaders to publicly campaign for a reduction of the heat in our public life, there would be positive consequences. In fact, there are some well-publicized hints about how our elected representatives in Congress can "turn down the heat," as I noted in chapter 1 in describing their reaction to the shooting of Gabrielle Giffords. I can only hope that these attempts will continue. But "the action" has to be in the minds of individuals. That's us.

Summarizing: Improving Our Public Discourse—Principle Number Three

You can control your emotions. You do not have to let yourself get stirred up by the extremist speech of our public radical speakers. Be mindful of their attempts to spread divisiveness and polarization among the citizenry.

4. Go Slower

We know that when people are making judgments about attitudes and beliefs, the more strongly emotionally committed to the issue they are, the faster they make their judgments. They "rush to judge." To cut down on radical hearing's effects, we should slow down and think carefully about what other people are saying, even if we dislike what they are saying. In fact, especially then. If someone wants to publically proclaim the good aspects of their ideas, then that radical-supporting speech is no problem for the rest of us. If Texas or Oklahoma football fans claim that "we're number one" and wave their index fingers in the television cameras, that is fine for them. But in actual fact I do not think that it matters all that much to, let's say, Vermont voters. Football fans' ego-involvement really has little or no impact on the larger social order. When, however, people use radical-attacking speech to deliberately try to cause dissension, fights, and wars (even if between rival football fans), then in principle it can be a social problem. Magnified by national television, radio, newspapers, and blogs, we have social polarization. Can we slow things down when radical-attacking speakers attempt to spread their fanaticism? If we think through how damaging they are trying to be, then we can more clearly think of alternative ways of responding. It is generally not a good idea to make a quick decision in the grip of hot-button emotions. Cool, rational deliberation about what you are hearing and careful making of important distinctions and comparisons is a key process in our principles of judgment, and this kind of deliberation can be an open pathway to a more unified society. It is likely that it will make for less upset for you personally.

Summarizing: Improving Our Public Discourse—Principle Number Four

Hearing and thinking about what other people believe can be, and should be, a careful, rational process. Take a lot of time to make careful and deliberate judgments about the attitudes and beliefs of others. Don't be so judgmental, and don't rush your judgment because of your emotions, even if you have trouble setting them aside.

5. Open Up Your Mind: Assimilation Contrast and the "Latitudes"

Beware of *confirmation bias.* Remember the Taber and Lodge study in which research participants were presented with the chance to view paragraphs arguing in support of either side of two hot topics, affirmative action and gun control. Those participants who were the strongest supporters of those topics were selectively biased in what they chose to read. Supporting the concept of *confirmation bias,* they overwhelmingly chose to view the statements supporting their own side of the issue while rejecting the opportunity to view the opposing side.

And beware of the disconfirmation bias: the tendency to be overly hostile and rejecting of evidence that contradicts one's beliefs. When judging the strength of the arguments made about both sides, emotionally involved participants rated the arguments on the opposite side of the issues as weaker, while they rated the arguments on their own side of the issue as stronger. Other studies we reviewed showed that biased partisans felt that their side was fairer, less biased, and truer than their opponents' side. Opposing points of view just do not get traction for an emotionally involved person.

These effects accompany the tendency of strongly committed people to easily reject others' statements of opinion because their extreme personal stance leads them to judge most statements as representing the opposite of their own beliefs. This is the contrast effect. At the same time, strongly committed people accept few statements into their own opinion stance, setting a high bar for an assimilation effect. Finally, they have a tendency to judge nearly all statements one way or the other, as either supportive or opposed to their strongly held points of view, resulting in a small latitude of noncommitment. Every statement gets judged, and nothing can be left in the ambiguous realm of moderate speech.

All beliefs should be considered fairly and openly, but the harsh reality of a radicalized society is that they are not. Voices of moderation are being lost, but middle-of-the-road beliefs are critical to establishing harmony, and it is important that they be heard. The latitudes are a vivid demonstration of black-and-white, two-category thinking. Expressed in daily parlance, "If you are not for me, you are against me." Though this is not necessarily true, thinking so can turn out to make it so.

Summarizing: Improving Our Public Discourse—Principle Number Five

Your personal beliefs can be strengthened, not harmed, by embracing different points of view. Listen to them; give them a chance to be heard. Embrace diversity. Understanding others and their beliefs is a key ingredient to getting along with them. You do not have to love what others say, but you can learn from what they say; you will grow if you do.

6. Redefine Your Self

What we think of as our self, literally our concept of our self, is a key to how judgment processes get established in our own personal ways of thinking. But our self-identity can become biased and exert distorting effects on our judgment when it becomes attached to emotion-laden group membership and group labels. This is especially a problem when there are negative distinctions in judging others. Merely seeing someone else as different has been shown to be sufficient cause for treating that person differently and more negatively. Our social identities only magnify these problems when they are linked to extremist group labels.

The boys of the Robbers Cave summer camp, the Rattlers and Eagles, fought viciously as group members, as individuals upholding group labels that led the boys to fight for honor, for prestige, for dominance. History has too many examples of religious and political persecutions carried out in the name of group ideology. But that ideology has to be endorsed by the individual, and that is the key to radical hearing.

A person's identity need not be entirely or mostly built upon that person's group identity or label. One promising avenue for improving our social relations as individual persons would be to help people unlink their selves, their concepts of who they are as individuals, from their ingroup identities when those identities lead to engagement in hostilities that damage the greater good.

We know that ingroup/outgroup distinctions arise quickly in social interaction with "the other" and that these distinctions lead to derogation, aggression, and even war. Emotionally disconnecting one's self-identity from a group label when that label promotes discriminating, derogative, or destructive behavior should reduce or eliminate the tendencies to engage "the other" in counterproductive interactions. You may be a Republican or a Christian or a Muslim, but you are not your group label. You are a person, and you are part of the larger community of humanity. If your group identification harms your social relations with your fellow human beings, you can drop it.

Summarizing: Improving Our Public Discourse—Principle Number Six

Do not assume that you are invariably on the side of the angels. Expand your self-concept to allow the possibility that what you are doing is not necessarily the only way. Admit that you may be harming others. But you can gain self-pride by finding ways to help us "all get along."

7. Join Together

Research on the minimal group effect, such as the study involving the Phis and the Gammas, is disturbing because it shows how easily we can come to discriminate against someone simply because they come from a group that is simply different from ours. Some social theorists argue that bringing people together in mutually rewarding situations will eliminate this tendency. However, Sherif and his colleagues in the Robbers Cave study tried that. They brought the two warring groups together at mealtime and made arrangements for the boys to mingle and eat together. The result? The war between the groups was worse than ever; mealtime became just one more occasion for warring. Only when superordinate goals were introduced into the daily events, when cooperation was needed for the attainment of desirable goals that the boys could not obtain on their own, were the group boundaries dissolved and peace and friendship across group lines firmly established. In this kind of more-harmonious atmosphere, aggression is actually counterproductive, a hindrance to self-fulfillment. As the sociologist Lewis Coser[3] has noted, we can reduce ingroup-outgroup hostilities by dissolving the boundaries that separate us and melding groups into a more cohesive society.

In our current times, there are numerous superordinate goals that can reduce our divisiveness. Scarce and undrinkable water, unbreathable air, and uncontrollable viruses are genuine threats to all humanity (and the animal kingdom as well). The challenges of achieving solutions to these superordinate goals will cut down and just maybe eliminate the divisive effects of radical speech and radical hearing. After all, we really are all members of just one group, humans. We do not live on separate planets, one for "us" and one for "them." There is just one planet, and protecting it could be the biggest superordinate goal of all. We have a common goal, maintaining the livability of the planet for the one big "us." Getting everyone to realize that fact is our next frontier. We should start that process by personally endorsing the principles I have presented in this book.

Summarizing: Improving Our Public Discourse—Principle Number Seven

Raise your sights. Incorporate into your life a set of goals greater than your own immediate views and beliefs. Contributing to a greater cause makes getting along with others a key to improving all of our lives and the lives of future generations.

WILL THESE SUGGESTIONS BE ADOPTED?

No matter how good a suggestion is, there is no guarantee that it will be taken to heart and actually adopted. People experience inertia in their patterns of thought and behavior, so we have to rationally speculate here about what barriers exist that might hinder people from adopting the suggestions presented in this chapter. No matter how solidly grounded in research a suggestion might be, people will have their own reasons for paying attention or actually accepting or rejecting the recommendations presented in this chapter. Some reasons why these suggestions may not be adopted are presented in the final chapter of this book. Interestingly, the very principles that have been reviewed provide some hints about forces that will likely lead people to resist making the changes I have suggested to counter radical hearing.

CHAPTER 10
CAN'T CHANGE OR WON'T CHANGE? THAT IS THE QUESTION

I n this book I presented an anatomy of radical hearing. I described it, diagnosed its underlying principles, and suggested ways that those principles could be used to eliminate it. In doing this, I reviewed many different examples of judgment processes in the context of hot-button political, religious, and social issues. Note, though, that what superficially looked like different political and social issues, are actually closely linked in terms of the principles underlying the way people react to those issues. In all instances, there was convergence on the same underlying theme: cognitively simple thinking and a loss of the ability to hear and accept voices of moderation. I even provided a diagnostic checklist in chapter 7 so that readers could easily identify radical hearing in their daily living. In chapter 9, I showed how those principles could be used as guidelines for reversing the effects of radical hearing. So, speaking in medical terms, I described the problem, gave a diagnosis, and recommended a specific course of therapeutic treatment to cure it.

In an ideal world, someone who is exposed to radical speech would read this book, learn how to recognize radical speech (using the checklist I presented in chapter 7) and then take to heart the seven principles for counteracting it; in that ideal world, people would follow those suggestions and radical hearing would be eliminated from our public discourse. Logically, this glorious outcome would undercut the divisiveness and polarization we are now experiencing; voices of moderation would once again be heard in the land, and we would unify our society. In his insightful new book, *Our Divided Political Heart*, E. J. Dionne traces two major themes in American history. Briefly stated, these themes are our drive toward individualistic goals and our countervailing motivation toward collective well-being.[1] Our current polarization reflects an imbalance toward the individualistic, and he proposes that we strive toward a better balance. If we could succeed at this, we could then achieve a better focus on solving our common problems rather than wasting so much effort trying to marginalize the people whose beliefs are different from our own.

Note that I just used the word logically. The wonderful outcome I have just described is the logical outcome we should expect to see if people were to follow the seven principles described in chapter 9. In fact, in some impressive ways we could be optimistic about our future. After all, the world has established the United Nations, a forum for all nations to come together, deliberate, and achieve the common good. It is intended to be a force for world peace and prosperity. We have an International Criminal Court at The Hague for enforcing universally accepted laws. We have the North Atlantic Treaty Organization (NATO), and we have the European Union. In America, the Supreme Court in 1954 ruled that separate educational facilities are inherently unequal facilities and that the Constitution mandates equal treatment for all. Also, there are many government and private nongovernmental entities that encourage intergroup cooperation. Antidiscrimination and diversity mandates are now part and parcel of how local governments regulate citizen affairs. As I reported in chapter 1, in response to the shooting of Congresswoman Gabrielle Giffords, the University of Arizona has announced the founding of a National Institute for Civil Discourse, where scholars and public-policy experts will be able to combine their strengths in pursuit of the goal of improving the level of our public discourse. These are encouraging developments, and there are many others too numerous to list.

Frankly, though, as helpful as these developments may be, they are not based on the scientific principles of human-judgment processes that I presented in this book. They seem to have grown more or less haphazardly, often in response to some crisis rather than as the result of cool and rational deliberation. I do not see any strong evidence of explicit reliance on scientific principles in these developments

And there remains one big elephant in the room. As any physician will tell you, it is common for people to fail in following through with the recommendations of their physicians. And if they actually do start what was recommended, they usually quit before they have completed the treatment. As in so many aspects of life, people do not always do what is good for them. I have to face the same issue here. What if people do not follow the seven suggestions I presented in chapter 9? Will the patient get better if people ignore this doctor's orders and fail to change their ways according to those seven principles?

In fact, we can use the general concepts from our review of radical hearing to track down and investigate closely the sources of resistance to change. If there is likelihood that many people will choose not to follow my suggestions, we should at least try to speculate about why they might not follow them. But I can provide more than just random speculation. In reviewing the topics I have discussed in this book, it becomes clear that there are two general domains of factors involved in radical hearing. They are: (1) cognitive factors in judgment processes, and (2) social processes in dealing with "the other." At a general level, there are two major sources of resistance to changing our ways. They are neatly captured in these two seemingly simple claims:

1. People don't change because they can't change.
2. People don't change because they won't change.

COGNITIVE FACTORS: WHY *CAN'T* PEOPLE CHANGE?

In chapter 2, I provided a framework for how it is that people become radical hearers. An essential aspect of the model I proposed is that people are not forced to hear extremist speech, at least not in advanced societies nor under the thumb of dictators who force their opinions and their style of governing upon a resisting populace. The model I proposed emphasizes that people make a free choice to hear that speech. The very fact of having made a free choice gives their experience with extremist speech high personal value; we value what we choose and, of course, we choose what we value. This combination leads to personal commitment to that speech, and that commitment leads to adoption of the speech into the individual's self-concept. This embeddedness and connectivity gives the self-system great rigidity and resistance to change, as Jack Brehm has shown with his concept of psychological reactance, which I presented in chapter 2. The psychological rigidity that results from this embeddedness and commitment to freely chosen behavior can become so great that, for example, the members of Rev. Jim Jones's People's Temple ended up participating in mass suicide because they could not break the bonds of their prior commitments.

An entirely new angle on extremism and beliefs is just now coming into view. Political science researchers have teamed up with physiologically oriented researchers, particularly in the field of genetics, and they are discovering that there may well be genetic contributions to extremism. Christopher Dawes and James Fowler[2] have shown that being associated with partisan beliefs is related to genetic alleles of the dopamine receptor. This may be a stable genetic correlate of the tendency to join in political groups and the persistence of partisan behavior over time. In other studies, researchers have employed data from twin studies to show that similarities in partisanship are more pronounced in identical twins than in nonidentical twins.[3,4] There is also new research by Douglas Oxley and his colleagues[5] showing that physiological reactivity, such as the startle reflex and responses to visual stimulation, is related to strong political beliefs. So if there are genetic underpinnings to our political beliefs, it may also be true of religious beliefs, another of our hot-button issues that cause social divisiveness. This is very new research, and much more needs to be learned about the physical inheritance and the strength of our partisanship, but the data so far are entirely consistent with what we know about the basic foundations of our judgment processes and the deep-seated and rigid aspects of radical hearing as I conceive of it.

In terms of judgment processes and emotional involvement, the studies I have presented here show that, as a consequence of adopting a radical hearing stance to one or more hot-button issues, radical hearers develop a simple, black-and-white, two-category cognitive system for viewing their world. As I discussed in chapter 5, their emotional commitments to their own personal point of view result in a lowered threshold for rejecting opposing ideas and a raised threshold for accepting any different ideas. They have wide latitudes of rejection and small latitudes of acceptance. In combination, these emotionally based judgments leave them no categories for accepting moderate, middle-of-the road, opinions and beliefs; they simply cannot hear voices of moderation. Their cognitive systems are relatively impoverished, and they show patterns of cognitive simplicity such as quick decision making and low effort spent on careful deliberation. Furthermore, biased people think that points of view opposite to their own are biased and untrue, and they reject the opportunity to even expose themselves to those other points of view. Their minds are made up, and they will not incorporate viewpoints other than their own. In fact, they experience psychological reactance against viewpoints other than their own. Without functional categories for understanding shades of opinion and middle-of-the-road opinions, they are very unlikely to change their ways. And as I discussed in chapter 1, they also demonstrate intolerance of ambiguity, preferring the cognitive comfort of certitude, authoritarianism, and discrimination against different others. A lay description of this syndrome would be cognitive laziness or, more technically, "least cognitive effort." In general, then, you should not expect biased, attitudinally committed partisans to have flexible, open-minded approaches to their world since they just do not have the judgment categories that would make such approaches possible.

These processes all become compounded when there is a social-identity issue. Merely being in a group different from another one is sufficient to lead to discrimination against the outgroup. As we saw earlier, the Phis discriminated against the Gammas even though there had been no interaction with the other group, since the other group was entirely fictional. Moreover, competition against people outside of one's own group has the effect of increasing the emotional commitment to one's ingroup. The ingroup-outgroup identities of the Rattlers and Eagles in the Robbers Cave study developed into hostile group interactions that eventually led to war. But in such circumstances, the self sees war as justified. Those boys developed a "my way or the highway" identity, and in this case they saw no other approach besides trying to harm the other campers in "their" campground. It took the introduction of seven superordinate goals before the rigid group boundaries were dissolved enough that the boys could come to accept each other as compatriots. The Robbers Cave study provides a good insight into much of human history. Past battles are rife with such self-identity processes. Engaging in the mutually beneficial goal-directed activities eventually eliminated the problems by leading the boys to redefine their identities toward a more inclusive, "let's all cooperate" sense of group identity.

If radical hearers are going to be expected to follow the suggestions in chapter 9, if people are to ever change their biased judgment processes, they will have to devote cognitive resources to implement the changes I recommended. But the data suggest that they do not have the cognitive resources or open-minded social identities needed for successfully making the suggested changes. I have just presented a book's worth of evidence explaining why it is that radical hearers cannot choose to change their minds. Given the cognitive and social props upon which their beliefs are formed and operate, the highly ego-involved are unlikely to make any changes to move toward a more moderate stance in their beliefs. But the Robbers Cave boys eventually gave up their hates and their wars and their self-labels as Rattlers and Eagles when they learned to cooperate with each other in the service of achieving superordinate goals. This model of change is quite clear, and it is well founded in research evidence, so it is now up to us to adopt the changes I recommended in chapter 9. It is our choice—our free choice.

EMOTIONAL FACTORS: WHY *WON'T* PEOPLE CHANGE?

I have just listed cognitive reasons for rigidity in radical hearing. But we also know from the research of Robert Zajonc, which I discussed in chapter 2, that "affect is primary." Our nervous system processes stimulus inputs by first funneling sensory information through the spinal cord and up through the brain stem and the back of the brain before finally processed it in the frontal lobes; that brain region is where our more rational thinking processes occur. As a consequence of this structural aspect of the human nervous system, we literally have emotional feelings about an input before it even gets to our conscious mind to process it. We like or dislike something even before we "know" what it is. Emotions are to a considerable degree primitive, basic, and hardwired. Given their very nature, they should be difficult to change.

In his insightful new book about polarization, Jonathan Haidt[6] speaks about the "elephant in the room," which I mentioned earlier in this chapter. This "elephant" is the predominance of emotional automatic processing that operates intuitively as we confront a particular situation. In this model, intuitive emotional reasoning sets the stage for our later conscious, rational processing that justifies the emotion-based decisions already made. In short, we emotionally intuit what kind of response we want to make, and then we justify our response with more formal logical reasoning. We intuitively like or dislike something, such as a political or religious belief, and then we justify our assessment of that belief with our more conscious thinking and justifying capacities. If this is to change, then we have to change the way the elephant does it work.

Of course there are instances in which people do experience

changes in their emotions. Such experiences as a severe trauma, a sudden religious conversion, and undergoing psychotherapy are major life changes that could make some fundamental emotional changes more likely to occur. And of course, people can willingly make efforts to change their emotions; that's why they voluntarily seek psychotherapy, for instance. But they have to want to make the change, and that wanting is the mysterious key to getting the process of change started. That desire to change would have to come after the emotional arousal coming from the hot-button topic has already arisen, and that is difficult to imagine.

As scientists, we really do not have a good handle on what might be the key components to wanting to change one's emotional commitments. From the logic of the principles of judgment, to change oneself enough to want to change one's commitments would imply (again, *logically imply*) that cognitions can win out over emotions. One should be a skeptic about the likelihood of such a condition coming about.

We can use some of our previous discussion to analyze this more closely. To make my point, go back to figure 4.1 in chapter 4. That figure displayed the judgment processes of strongly "antiblack" and strongly "problack" judges. Note that the data were separated into graphs within each group of judges: those who showed simple category systems of three categories, and those who showed more open, six-category judgments. From the usual judgment model, you would predict that those judges who used six categories would not show judgmental bias because they had more open, more complex reference scales. But in fact they did not show such a pattern. Even using six categories to judge the issue statements, the strongly problack judges still showed the usual contrast effect. Most of the statements were judged as being opposed to their own stand and were therefore judged into their latitudes of rejection. So these emotionally involved participants still showed judgmental bias. In spite of their ability to differentiate more finely among the positions being represented in the attitude statements, they still missed the middle-of-the-range, moderate statements. Here again, emotions dominated cognitions.

Emotions are motivational, not logical. So even though an emotionally involved person might know about bias, they still might not want to do anything about it. We like our emotions; they are a key part of who we are, especially when we get ego-involved with our beliefs. We love what we love and we hate what we hate, and we generally have little reason to want to make a change in the balance of that equation. Hating something is easy, and loving it is wonderfully comforting. Changing one's emotional commitments is one the most formidable challenges a person can face. Most of us would not willingly choose to make a change. The principles I presented in chapter 9 show us the way to go, but there is no research to show how to turn a person toward engaging them.

ANY SOLUTIONS?

I have raised two important considerations about where we can go from here. Consider this angle on the problem. We live in a society in which everyone is guaranteed freedom of speech. So the problem of social divisiveness and polarized politics does not lie with radical speakers; they are free to have their say, and we cannot, and should not, infringe on their freedom to say whatever they want to say. But following that same logic, there must also be freedom of hearing; we are free to listen to anybody. And the logical corollary to that is that we also have freedom of endorsement. We can endorse, or reject, any speech we want to. In short, people can choose to be a radical hearer, or they can choose not to be a radical hearer. I hope that the topics I have presented in this book will tilt the odds toward moving away from our radical hearing rather than continuing on the path of our current, destructive ways. Clearly this is an issue in serious need of scientific investigation. Doing that research, and applying it in our daily lives, is now up to all of us.

NOTES

INTRODUCTION. RADICAL SPEECH/RADICAL HEARING: WHY VOICES OF MODERATION CAN'T BE HEARD

1. Quoted in Evil Theists, http://eviltheists.com/religious-extremists/149-gary-potter-catholics-for-christian-political-action (accessed June 7, 2012).

2. Quoted at an antiabortion rally in Fort Wayne, Indiana, *Fort Wayne News Sentinel*, August 16, 1993.

3. Quoted in Ian Curtis, *Jesus: Myth or Reality?* (iUniverse, 2006).

4. James Madison, *Memorial and Remonstrances against Religious Assessments*, pamphlet 17, para. 7, Address to the General Assembly of the Commonwealth of Virginia, 1785.

5. Thomas Jefferson, letter to Horatio G. Spafford, March 17, 1814.

6. Amos Tversky and Daniel Kahneman, "Judgment under Uncertainty: Heuristics and Biases," *Science* 185 (1974): 1124–31.

7. Malcolm Gladwell, *Blink: The Power of Thinking without Thinking* (New York: Little, Brown, 2005).

8. Daniel Kahneman, *Thinking, Fast and Slow* (New York: Farrar, Straus, and Giroux, 2011).

9. Susan T. Fiske and Shelley E. Taylor, *Social Cognition*, 2nd ed. (New York: McGraw-Hill, 1991), p. 394.

10. William Golding, *Lord of the Flies* (New York: Coward-McCann, 1962).

CHAPTER 1. DELIBERATE DIVISIVENESS

1. *Arizona Daily Star* editorial, January 9, 2011.

2. Paul Krugman, "Climate of Hate," *New York Times*, January 9, 2011, http://www.nytimes.com/2011/01/10/opinion/10krugman.html (accessed June 11, 2012).

3. Barack Obama, "State of the Union" address, January 25, 2011.

4. David Lightman and William Douglas, "Compromise Tough in D.C.," *Arizona Republic*, May 22, 2011.

5. Robyn Stryker, *National Institute of Civil Discourse Research Brief 6: Political polarization* (Tucson: University of Arizona, 2011), p. 8.

6. Lightman and Douglas, "Compromise Tough in D.C."

7. John Avlon, *Wingnuts: How the Lunatic Fringe is Hijacking America* (New York: Beast Books, 2010).

8. Ibid.

9. Attributed to Rush Limbaugh, http://www.boycottliberalism.com/Rush-Limbaugh-quotes.htm.

10. *Rush Limbaugh* television show, October 9, 2008.

11. Ann Coulter, *Treason: Liberal Treachery from the Cold War to the War on Terrorism* (New York: Crown Forum), p. 203.

12. Keith Olbermann, *Truth and Consequences: Special Comments on the Bush Administration's War on American Values* (New York: Random House, 2007), p. 7.

13. Franklin Delano Roosevelt radio address to the American people, October 26, 1931.

14. James Russell Lowell, *The Writings of James Russell Lowell: Literary Essays* (New York: Houghton Mifflin, 1890).

15. Ralph Waldo Emerson: *Essays: Second Series* (Boston: J. Munroe, 1844).

16. Robert F. Kennedy, *The Pursuit of Justice*, ed. Theodore J. Lowi (New York: Harper & Row, 1964), pp. 68–69.

17. Pat Buchanan, speech presented to the Christian Coalition, September 1993.

18. King George III, First Address to the English Parliament, October 27, 1775.

19. Theodore Roosevelt, letter to S. Stanwood Menken, chairman of the Committee on Congress of Constructive Patriotism, January 10, 1917.

20. Eberhard Jackel, *Hitler's World View: A Blueprint for Power* (Middletown, CT: Harvard University Press, 1981), citing a speech at Nuremberg, Germany, January 13, 1923.

21. Rev. Fred Phelps, quoted in the *State Press*, Arizona State University, March 11, 1998.

22. Westboro Baptist Church press release, September 7, 1998.

23. Henry Morris, *The Remarkable Birth of Planet Earth* (Minneapolis: Dimension Books, 1972).

24. Pat Robertson, *The 700 Club* television show, April 9, 1991.

25. Pat Robertson, fundraising letter, cited on Positive Atheism, 1992, http://www.positiveatheism.org. Reported in the *New York Times*, August 26, 1992.

26. Robert Ingersoll, *The Works of Robert G. Ingersoll, Vol. 5 (of 12) Dresden Edition—Discussions* (New York: Dresden, 1905).

27. Friedrich Nietzsche, "Why I Am a Destiny," in *Ecce Homo* (New York: Oxford University Press, 1888).

28. Stephen J. Gould, *Bully for Brontosaurus: Reflections in Natural History* (New

York: Norton, 1991), quoted in James A. Haught, *2000 Years of Disbelief: Famous People with the Courage to Doubt* (Amherst, NY: Prometheus Books, 1996).

29. Interview with Richard Dawkins, reported in *Sunday Telegraph* (UK), September 26, 1999.

CHAPTER 2. THE PSYCHOLOGY OF BECOMING COMMITTED

1. Jack Brehm, *A Theory of Psychological Reactance* (New York: Academic Press, 1966).

2. Stephen Worchel and Jack Brehm, "Effect of Threats to Attitudinal Freedom as a Function of Agreement with the Communicator," *Journal of Personality and Social Psychology* 14 (1970): 18–22.

3. Jack Brehm and Ann Cole, "Effect of a Favor which Reduces Freedom," *Journal of Personality and Social Psychology* 3 (April 1966): 420–26.

4. J. W. Reich and Alex J. Zautra, "Life Events and Personal Causation: Some Relationships with Satisfaction and Distress," *Journal of Personality and Social Psychology* 41 (November 1981): 1002–12.

5. James M. Henslin, "Craps and Magic," *American Journal of Sociology* 73 (November 1967): 316–30.

6. Ellen Langer, "The Illusion of Control," *Journal of Personality and Social Psychology* 32 (1975): 311–28.

7. Ibid, p. 316.

8. H. R. Arkes et al., "The Psychology of Windfall Gains," *Organizational Behavior and Human Decision Processes* 59 (September 1994): 331–47.

9. Ibid.

10. Daniel Kahneman, *Thinking, Fast and Slow* (New York: Farrar, Straus and Giroux, 2011).

11. Leon Festinger, Henry Riecken, and Stanley Schachter, *When Prophecy Fails* (Minneapolis: University of Minnesota Press, 1956).

12. Neal Osherow, "Making Sense of the Nonsensical," in *Readings about the Social Animal*, ed. Elliot Aronson (New York: Macmillan, 2003).

13. Robert Cialdini, *Influence: Science and Practice*, 4th ed. (Boston: Allyn & Bacon, 2001).

14. Douglas T. Kenrick, Steven Neuberg, and Robert Cialdini, *Social Psychology: Unraveling the Mystery* (Boston: Allyn & Bacon, 2005), p. 142.

15. Eva M. Pomerantz, Shelly Chaiken, and Rosalind Tordesillas, "Attitude Strength and Resistance Processes," *Journal of Personality and Social Psychology* 69 (September 1995): 408–19.

16. Christopher T. Dawes, James H. Fowler "Partisanship, Voting, and the Dopamine D2 Receptor, *Journal of Politics* 71 (2009): 1157–71.

17. James H. Fowler, Laura A. Baker, and Christopher T. Dawes, "Genetic Variation in Political Participation, *American Political Science Review* 102 (2008): 233–48.

18. William A. Scott, "Structure of Natural Cognitions," *Journal of Personality and Social Psychology* 12 (August 1969): 261–78.

19. Patricia W. Linville, "Self-Complexity and Affective Extremity: Don't Put All of Your Eggs in One Cognitive Basket," *Social Cognition* 3 (1985): 94–120.

20. Marc J. Hetherington and Jonathan Weiler, *Authoritarianism and Polarization in American Politics* (New York: Cambridge University Press, 2009).

21. Philip E. Tetlock, "Personality and Isolationism: Content Analysis of Senatorial Speeches," *Journal of Personality and Social Psychology* 41 (1981): 737–43.

22. Philip E. Tetlock, "Cognitive Style and Political Belief Systems in the British House of Commons," *Journal of Personality and Social Psychology* 46 (1984): 365–75.

23. O. J. Harvey, David E. Hunt, and Harold M. Schroder, *Conceptual Systems and Personality Organization* (New York: Wiley, 1961).

24. B. Jack White and O. J. Harvey, "Effects of Personality and Own Stand on Judgment and Production of Statements about a Central Issue," *Journal of Experimental Social Psychology* 1 (October 1965): 334–47.

25. Charles G. Lord, Lee Ross, and Mark Lepper, "Biased Assimilation and Attitude Polarization: The Effects of Prior Theories on Subsequently Considered Evidence," *Journal of Personality and Social Psychology* 37 (1979): 2098–2109.

26. Ziva Kunda, "The Case for Motivated Reasoning" *Psychological Bulletin* 103 (November 1990): 480–98.

27. Robert B. Zajonc, "On the Primacy of Affect," *American Psychologist* 39 (1984): 117–23.

28. Paul Slovic et al., "The Affect Heuristic," in *Heuristics and Biases: The Psychology of Intuitive Judgment*, ed. Thomas Gilovich, Dale Griffin, and Daniel Kahneman (Cambridge: Cambridge University Press, 2002).

29. Charles S. Taber and Milton Lodge, "Motivated Skepticism in the Evaluation of Political Beliefs," *American Journal of Political Science* 50 (2006): 755–69.

30. Pomerantz, Chaiken, and Tordesillas, "Attitude Strength and Resistance Processes."

CHAPTER 3. JUDGING AND (MIS)PERCEIVING THE WORLD

1. Margaret Tresselt, "The Effect of the Experiences of Contrasted Groups upon the Formation of a New Scale of Judgment," *Journal of Social Psychology* 27 (1948): 209–16.

2. Gustav T. Fechner, *Elements of Psychophysics*, trans. Helmut E. Adler, ed. Davis H. Howes and Edwin G. Boring (New York: Holt, Rinehart and Winston, 1966).

3. Muzafer Sherif, Daniel Taub, and Carl I. Hovland, "Assimilation and Contrast Effects of Anchoring Stimuli on Judgments," *Journal of Experimental Psychology* 55 (February 1958): 150–55; Tresselt, "Effect of the Experiences of Contrasted Groups."

4. Sherif, Taub, and Hovland, "Assimilation and Contrast Effects."

5. Adapted by the author from ibid.

6. Adapted by the author from ibid.

7. Donald R. Brown, "Stimulus-Similarity and the Anchoring of Subjective Scales," *American Journal of Psychology* 66 (1953): 199–213.

8. Ibid., p. 208.

9. Donald M. Johnson, "Generalization of a Scale of Values by the Averaging of Practice Effects," *Journal of Experimental Psychology* 34 (1944): 425–36.

10. Ibid., p. 436.

11. Douglas T. Kenrick and Sara E. Gutierres, "Contrast Effects and Judgments of Physical Attractiveness: When Beauty Becomes a Social Problem," *Journal of Personality and Social Psychology* 38 (1980): 131–40.

12. Pat Robertson, fundraising letter, 1992, reported in the *New York Times*, August 26, 1992, http://www.nytimes.com/1992/08/26/us/Robertson-letter -attacks-feminists.html (accessed July 11, 2012).

CHAPTER 4. EMOTIONS, ATTITUDES, AND JUDGMENT PROCESSES

1. David Hume, *A Treatise of Human Nature* (New York: Dover, 2003).

2. Louis Leon Thurstone and E. J. Chave, *The Measurement of Attitude: A Psychophysical Method and Some Experiments with a Scale for Measuring Attitude toward the Church* (Chicago: University of Chicago Press, 1929).

3. Ibid.

4. Ibid.

5. Ibid.

6. Adapted by the author from ibid. Copyright 1929 by the University of Chicago. All rights reserved. Published 1929. Eighth impression 1966. Printed in the United States of America.

7. Adapted by the author from ibid. Copyright 1929 by the University of Chicago. All rights reserved. Published 1929. Eighth impression 1966. Printed in the United States of America.

8. Marvin E. Shaw and Jack M. Wright, *Scales for the Measurement of Attitudes* (New York: McGraw-Hill, 1967).

CHAPTER 5. WHEN ATTITUDES AND THE SELF GET INVOLVED

1. Carl I. Hovland and Muzafer Sherif, "Judgmental Phenomena and Scales of Attitude Measurement: Item Displacement in Thurstone Scales," *Journal of Abnormal and Social Psychology* 47 (October 1952): 822–32.

2. Ibid.

3. Adapted by the author from ibid.

4. Muzafer Sherif and Carl I. Hovland, "Judgmental Phenomena and Scales of Attitude Measurement: Placement of Items with Individual Choice of Number of Categories," *Journal of Abnormal and Social Psychology* 48 (January 1953): 135–41.

5. Ibid.

6. Adapted by the author from ibid.

7. Muzafer Sherif and Carl Hovland, *Social Judgment* (New Haven, CT: Yale University Press).

8. Ibid.

9. Ibid.

10. Ibid.

11. Adapted by the author from ibid.

12.. Alice H. Eagly and Shelly Chaiken, *The Psychology of Attitudes* (Fort Worth, TX: Harcourt Brace Jovanovich, 1993).

13. Carolyn W. Sherif, Muzafer Sherif, and Roger E. Nebergall, *Attitude and Attitude Change* (Philadelphia: W. B. Saunders, 1965).

14. Adapted by the author from ibid.

CHAPTER 6. OTHER ISSUES, OTHER EFFECTS, STILL THE SAME PRINCIPLE

1. James M. Smallwood and Steven K. Gragert, eds., *Will Rogers' Daily Telegram*, vol. 1, *The Coolidge years, 1926–1929* (Stillwater: Oklahoma State University Press, 1978).

2. C. I. Hovland, O. J. Harvey, and Muzafer Sherif, "Assimilation and Contrast Effects in Communication and Attitude Change," *Journal of Abnormal and Social Psychology* 55 (1957): 242–52.

3. Adapted by the author from ibid.

4. Alvar O. Elbing, "An Experimental Investigation of the Influence of Reference Group Identification on Role Playing as Applied to Business" (PhD diss., University of Washington, 1963).

5. Ibid.

6. Adapted by the author from ibid.

7. John W. Reich, "Ego-Involvement as a Factor in Attitude Assessment by the Own Categories Technique" (master's thesis, University of Oklahoma), referenced in John W. Reich and Muzafer Sherif, Report of Institute of Group Relations, 1963.

8. Adapted by the author from ibid.

9. Robert B. Zajonc, "On the Primacy of Affect," *American Psychologist* 39 (1984): 117–23.

10. Hovland, Harvey, and Sherif, "Assimilation and Contrast Effects."

11. Adapted by the author from ibid.

12. Ibid.

13. Carolyn W. Sherif and Norman Jackman, "Judgments of Truth in Collective Controversy," *Public Opinion Quarterly* 30 (1966): 173–86.

14. Charles S. Taber and Milton Lodge, "Motivated Skepticism in the Evaluation of Political Beliefs," *American Journal of Political Science* 50 (2006): 755–69.

15. Alice H. Eagly and Shelly Chaiken, *The Psychology of Attitudes* (Fort Worth, TX: York: Harcourt Brace Jovanovich, 1993).

16. Carolyn W. Sherif et al., "Personal Involvement, Social Judgment, and Action," *Journal of Personality and Social Psychology* 27 (1973): 311–23.

17. Robyn M. Dawes, David Singer, and Frank Lemons, "An Experimental Analysis of the Contrast Effect and Its Implications for Intergroup Communication and the Indirect Assessment of Attitude," *Journal of Personality and Social Psychology* 21 (March 1972): 281–95.

18. Ibid.

19. Ibid.

20. Robert P. Vallone, Lee Ross, and Mark R. Lepper, "The Hostile Media Phenomenon: Biased Perception and Perceptions of Media Bias in Coverage of the Beirut Massacre," *Journal of Personality and Social Psychology* 49 (1985): 577–85.

21. Ibid., pp. 584–85.

CHAPTER 8. OUR SOCIAL RELATIONS JUST MAGNIFY OUR BIASES

1. Anne Locksley, Vilma Ortiz, and Christine Hepburn, "Social Categorization and Discriminatory Behavior: Extinguishing the Minimal Intergroup Discrimination Effect," *Journal of Personality and Social Psychology* 39 (November 1980): 773–83.

2. Jacob M. Rabbie and Murray Horwitz, "Arousal of Ingroup-Outgroup Bias by a Chance Win or Loss," *Journal of Personality and Social Psychology* 13 (November 1969): 269–77.

3. "George Aiken quotes," ThinkExist.com, http://thinkexist.com/quotation/if_we_were_to_wake_up_some_morning_and_find_that/206784.html.

4. John Dollard et al., *Frustration and Aggression* (New Haven, CT: Yale University Press, 1939).

5. Joseph T. Hepworth and Stephen G. West, "Lynchings and the Economy: A Time-Series Reanalysis of Hovland and Sears (1940)," *Journal of Personality and Social Psychology* 55 (1988): 239–47.

6. Herbert C. Covey, Scott Menard, and Robert Franzese, *Juvenile Gangs*, 2nd ed. (Springfield, IL: Charles C. Thomas, 1997).

7. Tim Delaney, *American Street Gangs* (Upper Saddle River, NJ: Pearson, 2006).

8. Ibid., p. 152.

9. Muzafer Sherif et al., *The Robbers Cave Experiment: Intergroup Conflict and Cooperation* (Middletown, CT: Wesleyan University Press, 1988).

10. Lewis A. Coser, *The Functions of Social Conflict* (Glencoe, IL: Free Press, 1956).

11. Thomas Kuhn and Thomas McPartland, "An Empirical Investigation of Self-Attitudes," *American Sociological Review* 19 (1954): 68–76.

12. William James, *The Principles of Psychology* (New York: Holt, 1980), p. 294.

13. William Golding, *Lord of the Flies* (New York: Coward-McCann, 1962).

CHAPTER 9. SEVEN BASIC PRINCIPLES FOR RESTORING OUR UNITY

1. Jon Kabat-Zinn, *Full Catastrophe Living: Using the Wisdom of Your Body to Face Stress, Pain, and Illness* (New York: Dell, 1990).

2. Steven Hayes, Kirk D. Strosahl, and Kelly G. Wilson, *Acceptance and Commitment Therapy: An Experimental Approach to Behavior Change* (New York: Guilford Press, 1999).

3. Lewis A. Coser, *The Functions of Social Conflict* (Glencoe, IL: Free Press, 1956).

CHAPTER 10. CAN'T CHANGE OR WON'T CHANGE? THAT IS THE QUESTION

1. E. J. Dionne Jr., *Our Divided Political Heart* (New York: Bloomsbury, 2012).

2. Christopher T. Dawes and James H. Fowler, "Partisanship, Voting, and the Dopamine D2 Receptor," *Journal of Politics* 71 (2009): 1157–71.

3. Jaime E. Settle, Christopher T. Dawes, and James H. Fowler, "The Heritability of Partisan Attachment," *Political Research Quarterly* 62 (2009): 601–13;

4. James H. Fowler, Laura A. Baker, and Christopher T. Dawes, "Genetic Variation in Political Participation," *American Political Science Review* 102 (May 2008): 233–48.

5. Douglas. R. Oxley et al., "Political Attitudes Vary with Physiological Traits," *Science* 321, no. 5896 (September 2008): 1667–70.

6. Jonathan Haidt, *The Righteous Mind: Why Good People Are Divided by Politics and Religion* (New York: Pantheon, 2012).

INDEX